I0409191

BEYOND ECONOMICS

Unlocking Lasting Wealth With Bible Wisdom

EPHRAIM UNUIGBE (ACA)

BEYOND ECONOMICS

Unlocking Lasting Wealth With Bible Wisdom

Ephraim Unuigbe (ACA)

Contact the author via info@ephraim-unuigbe.com

DEDICATION

I dedicate this book to everyone on the journey of creating lasting wealth using bible principles.

TABLE OF CONTENTS

PREFACE

I often feel like an imposter because I have authored numerous books on personal finance and wealth creation, yet I struggle to apply these principles in my own life. While these principles have proven effective for millions of people, I grapple with a sense of inconsistency because I do not fully practice what I preach.

My background as an accountant and my extensive research contribute to the knowledge I share in my books. I draw upon my education and the experiences of others to provide valuable insights. However, it weighs on me that I possess knowledge about economic rules that I have not fully embraced in my personal life.

For instance, there are no economic principles advocating for allocating ten percent of income as tithe or making impulsive pledges or seeds without due diligence. Moreover, the concept of giving to receive, which I address in my books, does not align seamlessly with economic theories. These conflicts create a dilemma within me.

In my works, I advocate for principles like prioritizing self-savings, proportionate saving, wise investments, and giving to others or charitable causes with any surplus. However, in today's challenging economic climate, it is often difficult to have anything left over after meeting basic needs. The pressure to accumulate wealth makes it nearly impossible to fulfill the fundamental rule of wealth found in the Bible, which emphasizes giving to others.

To truly build lasting wealth, one may need to deviate from strict adherence to conventional economic principles. This book aims to uncover hidden secrets to wealth that have been overlooked due to their lack of popularity or applicability in our natural world. The insights shared will either open readers' eyes to new possibilities or reinforce truths they already hold dear in their hearts, aligning with what they believe God has revealed to them.

For Christian readers, the path to wealth-building may not strictly conform to conventional economic principles. Doubters need only look at historical and contemporary examples of individuals who have amassed significant wealth while disregarding these principles. Along the way, we seem to have strayed from our roots, following a different path akin to the actions of Cain, as described in Genesis 4:17, from which economic principles are derived.

This does not mean that wealth cannot be attained by following economic principles; indeed, many of the world's richest individuals have achieved success through such methods. However, true wealth, as described in Proverbs 10:22, is a gift from God, bestowed without sorrow. These individuals may withhold the secrets to their wealth, burdened by their own challenges.

If your aim is to build lasting wealth in this life while remaining faithful to Christ, it is crucial to follow God's principles rather than relying solely on economic strategies.

CHAPTER ONE

FOUNDATION OF WEALTH CREATION

CHAPTER ONE

FOUNDATION OF WEALTH CREATION

God wants us to be wealthy. There is a belief by many that being wealthy is a sin especially when Jesus mentioned that it is easier for a camel to go into the eyes of a needle that for a rich man to enter the kingdom of God. Matthew 19:21-24. If these verses of the scriptures are taken, it means no rich person will enter the kingdom, but this is not what Jesus meant otherwise, Abraham will not be in heaven or Job or Joseph because these people were all wealthy.

Scholars have debated the true meaning behind Jesus' statement about a camel and a needle. Some argue that Jesus may have been using a play on words, as the Aramaic word for "rope" was like the Greek word for "camel" mentioned in the verse. It is suggested that the word may have been misspelled, leading Jesus to make an analogy about threading a thick rope through the eye of a needle, illustrating something extremely difficult but not entirely impossible.

Alternatively, some propose that during that time, there existed a small gate called a "needle." Others maintain that Jesus intentionally used the absurdity of a literal interpretation involving camels and needles to emphasize his point.

While various interpretations exist regarding the specific meaning of camels and needles in Biblical times, they all convey the same underlying lesson: Jesus was highlighting the extreme difficulty, if not impossibility, for a rich person to enter the Kingdom of God.

In fact, when the disciples express their doubts about anyone being able to be saved,

Jesus responds, "With man this is impossible, but with God all things are possible" (Matthew 19:26).

Jesus himself settles the matter by affirming that he deliberately referred to something impossible, emphasizing the profound challenges faced by the wealthy in entering God's Kingdom.

What is the foundation of wealth?

The very first point in the bible where wealth was first mentioned was in Genesis 13, the story of Abraham (then known as Abram) and his nephew Lot unfolds. They both had acquired great wealth, including livestock and possessions, while living in the land of Canaan. "Now Abram was very rich in livestock, in silver, and in gold." This verse indicates that Abraham had acquired significant wealth in terms of livestock, silver, and gold.

Going back to where it all began, we see in Genesis 12 that it was God's idea to give wealth to Abraham from the very beginning.

Genesis chapter 12 from verse 1 to 3.

> *"1 Now the Lord had said unto Abram, Get thee out of thy country, and from thy kindred, and from thy father's house, unto a land that I will shew thee: 2 And I will make of thee a great nation, and I will bless thee, and make thy name great; and thou shalt be a blessing: 3 And I will bless them that bless thee, and curse him that curseth thee: and in thee shall all families of the earth be blessed."*

As we have observed above, in the promise that God made to Abraham, He included his children which is why as we see in the life of Isaac, this promise is also evident. In Genesis 26:12-14, it says,

> *12 Then Isaac sowed in that land, and received in the same year an hundredfold: and the Lord blessed him. 13 And the man waxed great, and went forward, and grew until he became very great: 14 For he had possession of flocks, and possession of herds, and great store of servants: and the Philistines envied him.*

The above passages are the result of God's word again of His assurance to make Isaac wealthy if you read from the beginning of that chapter of Genesis 26. The very same is replicated in the life of Jacob the Grandson of Abraham in Genesis 30:43,

43 And the man increased exceedingly, and had much cattle, and maidservants, and menservants, and camels, and asses.

Following from the many examples above from the lives of those God called, we can find other examples in the Bible that shows that the desire of God is to give wealth to men.

Below are a few examples:

- Proverbs 10:22: "The blessing of the Lord makes a person rich, and he adds no sorrow with it."
- Psalm 35:27: "Let them shout for joy and be glad, who favor my cause; let them say continually, 'The Lord be magnified, who has pleasure in the prosperity of his servant.'"

- Deuteronomy 8:18: "But you shall remember the Lord your God, for it is he who gives you power to get wealth, that he may confirm his covenant that he swore to your fathers, as it is this day."
- James 1:17: "Every good gift and every perfect gift is from above, coming down from the Father of lights, with whom there is no variation or shadow due to change."
- Matthew 6:33: "But seek first his kingdom and his righteousness, and all these things will be given to you as well." (Here, "all these things" refers to the necessities of life, including material provision.)

These are just a few examples of the many instances from the Bible that indicates God's ultimate desire to bless man. God's plans have not changed and continuing from the conversation in Matthew 19 from verse 27 to 30, we see Peter questioning Jesus about the prize for following Him. Jesus swiftly responded that in this life, they will receive a hundredfold and, in the world, to come eternal life. Jesus did not try to downplay this very important question to make it look like it was irrelevant. This only shows one thing, God is BIG on reward and makes the offer from the very beginning, so you know what you are up for.

This here is what differentiates our call to a wealthy place from the world. There is the afterlife reward and that is even more valuable in the scheme of things. Think about it deeply and you will realize that you may be able to enjoy earthly wealth for say a hundred years, but eternal wealth is forever, a world without end. When we have this understanding, the words in Luke 12 verse 34, begin to make sense, where it says, "For where your treasure is, there your heart will be also".

These passages convey the message that God is a generous and benevolent deity who takes pleasure in bestowing His people with good gifts. These blessings encompass not only material abundance, such as wealth, but also extend to various spiritual and emotional aspects like health, happiness, and peace.

However, it is crucial to bear in mind that the blessings from God are not solely focused on financial prosperity. They encompass a broader spectrum of provisions that enhance our well-being. Therefore, if you are seeking financial blessings from God, it is essential to acknowledge His generous nature and His willingness to bestow good gifts upon His people.

CHAPTER TWO

POSITIONING YOURSELF FOR WEALTH

CHAPTER TWO

POSITIONING YOURSELF FOR WEALTH

The fact that God wants you to be wealthy does not automatically mean you will be wealthy. Universally, there are rules to almost everything and God's rule to wealth is not an exception.

In this chapter we shall be zeroing in on the two important positioning for a lasting wealth creation and the positioning is evident all through the Bible. We shall only be discussing some examples to show us the importance of rightly positioning ourselves for God's promises of lasting wealth.

From Chapter One like we read in Genesis 12, the narration started in the middle of the story, because from verse 1 it says "... the Lord HAD..." meaning God already called Abraham before now and the promises made here. This is further evident from Acts 7: 2-3, the account of Stephen,

> *2 And he said, Men, brethren, and fathers, hearken; The God of glory appeared unto our father Abraham, when he was in Mesopotamia, before he dwelt in Charran, 3 And said unto him, Get thee out of thy country, and from thy kindred, and come into the land which I shall shew thee.*

We see from the above that Abraham was first called in Mesopotamia, and he was called alone, but he went to settle Harran and with his family. God came down again after Terah, his father had died. You will find this narration from Genesis 11:31-32 through to Genesis 12:1.

Perhaps God had called you too like He called Abraham, but you have hesitated or taken the convenient option. Perhaps you're grappling with the perplexity of why God would intentionally disrupt the seemingly well-ordered course of your life. Your family provides close support, and overall, things are going smoothly where you currently reside. However, just as God called Abraham, He might also be beckoning you towards a place of abundance. Yet, you may unknowingly hinder that divine call by opting for the convenient route or the path of least resistance.

It's possible to identify as a Christian without fully embracing the calling to a place of abundance, similar to Abraham's experience. The directive towards wealth is a personal call, not one that applies to everyone, and it is also dependent on location. This is a fundamental principle of wealth as outlined in the Bible. The business or career you intend to pursue must be situated in a specific place and tailored specifically for you. It's important to avoid following the crowd and instead focus on the individual instruction given by God. While Joseph's circumstances were unique and he lacked the freedom to choose his location, we are typically provided with specific instructions regarding our chosen careers or businesses and the corresponding geographical placement they require.

If your plan is to build lasting wealth according to Bible principles, you MUST learn to listen for the call, the call to a place and the call alone. The call of God to a place does not have to be the conventional way like we are used to, and this does not only apply to building wealth but also our assignment. Aside the popular examples of Abraham that we have discussed extensively in Genesis

12: 1, we also see this in the life of Isaac where God told him to remain in Gerar in Genesis 26:2. God also appeared to Moses in the burning bush to go to Egypt Exodus 3:1-10.

Another illustration is seen in the calling of John the Baptist. Although he was called before he was even born, his place of impact was unexpected - the wilderness. In those days, most religious individuals gathered in synagogues, not in desolate areas like the wilderness. It's possible that God has called you to a place where you feel uncomfortable because of others' opinions or because it doesn't align with societal expectations. However, the truth is that you won't begin to see the goodness in that place until you obey. A similar situation occurred with Abraham after he and Lot separated, leaving Abraham with what seemed to be an unproductive land. At this point, Abraham had gained a deeper understanding of God and how He could turn unfavorable circumstances to his advantage. We all know the outcome of that story, as described in Genesis 13.

God's call often beckons us to leave the comfort of the familiar and step into the unknown. Through His mercies and the guidance of His Spirit, God continues to call us towards new horizons. In our present world, we can observe numerous instances where individuals who have amassed wealth are compelled to relocate from bustling city centers to the outskirts. If you haven't yet heard that call, it suggests that you may not have aligned yourself with God's plan just yet.

The second principle to consider for experiencing supernatural positioning and God's blessings is what I would refer to as the doctrine of solitude or being a loner. We can observe this principle from the story of Abraham. Despite eventually obeying God's instructions regarding his location, Abraham initially journeyed with others - first with his father and later with his nephew Lot. As we later discover, Lot brought about trouble for Abraham, and if it hadn't been for God's intervention, Abraham could have suffered more than the loss of fertile land. However, God remained faithful throughout.

God's call is often meant for us individually. This doesn't imply that we cannot have business partners or be engaged in partnerships, but it is likely that on the path to wealth creation or fulfilling God's purpose, there will be seasons where we need to walk alone. This solitude allows us to fully embrace God's leading and discern His specific instructions for our lives.

When we align ourselves with these principles, we begin to witness the pieces falling into place. After Abraham and Lot went their separate ways, God revealed Himself to Abraham once more, reaffirming His promise to bless him and establish his descendants as a great nation. In Genesis 13:14-15, God spoke to Abraham, saying:

> *"Lift up your eyes and look from the place where you are, northward and southward and eastward and westward, for all the land that you see I will give to you and to your offspring forever."*

Obedience and lasting wealth are not mutually exclusive. In fact, they are essential to experiencing the supernatural. When we obey God, we open ourselves up to his blessings, which include both material and spiritual wealth.

Why God calls individuals?

God calls individuals alone. Although He tends to send people their way to help them achieve success, he ultimately calls individuals alone. We have already explained how God called Abraham and the iussue with carrying others along even when only him was called. This does not in any way mean that if you are married you must go without your wife or children. Again, like Abraham, his wife was not the problem because God sees Abraham and Sarah as one - Genesis

2:24 - *Therefore shall a man leave his father and his mother, and shall cleave unto his wife: and they shall be one flesh* .This is also why God has unhappy with Adam when he tried to separate himself from what Eve did in Genesis 3:12 - *And the man said, The woman whom thou gavest to be with me, she gave me of the tree, and I did eat.*

In the history of God calling through the ages, we see that He call them personally and not as a group. Same way when you got born again. You did not get born again by group decision. Even if you went out with others when the altar call was made, you made that decision by yourself for yourself because of the conviction you received in your spirit.

It is God's style to call individuals for many reasons and below are some of these reasons.

- To give them specific instructions about their assignment. God called Esther to be queen during a critical time to save the Jewish people from destruction (Esther 4:13-16).

- To express a unique quality of His personality. God calls Abraham to a life of righteousness and obedience. God called Abraham to leave his country and go to a land that God would show him, establishing a covenant and making him the father of many nations (Genesis 12:1-4).

- To show examples to others that one person is enough. God made the whole world from one man. See Genesis 1:26-28; Genesis 2:7, 21-25

- God calls individuals for spiritual transformation or salvation. Jesus called Zacchaeus, a tax collector, and as a result, he repented and experienced salvation (Luke 19:1-10)

- To give them a message for the people - God called Jeremiah to be a prophet to the nations, speaking His messages and calling people to repentance (Jeremiah 1:4-10).

- One of the main reasons and perhaps the most important is that God call is personal and individualistic because He wants us to grow in our relationship with him. He wants us to become more like him, and he uses our unique callings to help us do that. See below for a few examples.

  - Romans 8:29: "*For those whom he foreknew he also predestined to be conformed to the image of his Son, in order that he might be the firstborn among many brothers."*

- Ephesians 4:13: *"Until we all attain to the unity of the faith and of the knowledge of the Son of God, to mature manhood, to the measure of the stature of the fullness of Christ."*

- 1 John 3:2: *"Beloved, we are God's children now, and what we will be has not yet been revealed; but we know that when it is revealed we will be like him, for we will see him as he is."*

- Mark 3:13-14. It says: *And he went up on the mountain and called to him those he wanted, and they came to him. And he appointed twelve that they might be with him and that he might send them out to preach and to have authority to drive out demons.*

CHAPTER THREE

ESSENTIAL PRINCIPLES TO WEALTH CREATION

CHAPTER THREE

ESSENTIAL PRINCIPLES TO WEALTH CREATION

While other chapters are important, this chapter is the most important chapter you will read in this book. Here we delve into the obvious secret to building lasting wealth. This I believe is the main reason why you have this book in your hands.

Just in case you have not read the first two chapters of this book by applying the principles in this chapter alone, you may not get the desired result if you do not know the foundation of wealth creation – God, and positioning yourself righty by understanding that place where God wants you to be located physically, and why it's important that you are called alone as an individual.

Principle One - Obedience to God's instructions

Following from the above, we shall discuss the Biblical principles of wealth creation and will attempt to discuss the key fundamentals. As you may have noticed from the beginning of this book, we have anchored our discussions on the life of Abraham.

Aside from the instruction of the location of the call and that he goes alone, Abraham's call was pivoted on the principle of righteousness and obedience. Until Abraham totally obeyed God's instructions, he didn't get the full promise. However, God does not expect full obedience from His children. It is vital that you understand this, although God demands it, but He makes allowances for us to come to full obedience. In Genesis 12: 10 – 13,

10 And there was a famine in the land: and Abram went down into Egypt to sojourn there; for the famine was grievous in the land. 11 And it came to pass, when he was come near to enter into Egypt, that he said unto Sarai his wife, Behold now, I know that thou art a fair woman to look upon: 12 Therefore it shall come to pass, when the Egyptians shall see thee, that they shall say, This is his wife: and they will kill me, but they will save thee alive. 13 Say, I pray thee, thou art my sister: that it may be well with me for thy sake; and my soul shall live because of thee.

From here we see that Abraham has begun to obey God's command but not fully. He left Canaan to Egypt because of famine. This indicates that even when we are walking in God's divine plan, we will face challenges and it does not mean that God has left us, but He wants us to come to a realization that we trust Him completely despite our challenges. However, like Abraham, many of us would try to use our human wisdom to help ourselves out of the challenges by compromises most of the time. It is very unlikely that we can cope by ourselves without comprises outside the will of God.

Abraham's choice to leave Canaan leads to sin and this will lead to broken trust and disrupted relationships. Sins hurt us and everyone around us. But God is faithful even in our disobedience because He cannot deny Himself, 2 timothy 2 from verse 11 to 13 with 13 as the key emphases,

> *11 It is a faithful saying: For if we be dead with him, we shall also live with him: 12 If we suffer, we shall also reign*

with him: if we deny him, he also will deny us: 13 If we believe not, yet he abideth faithful: he cannot deny himself.

God's action to remain faithful in our disobedience is not an occasion to encourage us to remain in sin but that we should repent and return to Him. Let your sin when convicted draw you closer to God rather than away from Him. He is the only One that can help. I am sure you remember the parable of the Prodigal Son. The father was faithful and waiting patiently for the son to return home. We see this from the response of the father on the son's return.

In those times when you realize that you may have deviated from God's plan and purpose like Abraham, remind yourself that God is not surprised and that He is near. The point of the challenge that we may be facing is to strengthen our resolve on God to trust Him for what He said he will do.

Following from God's intervention in the life of Abraham in Egypt by preventing Pharaoh from having Sarah, see God's intervention in Genesis 12 from verse 16 to 19,

> *16 And he entreated Abram well for her sake: and he had sheep, and oxen, and he asses, and menservants, and maidservants, and she asses, and camels. 17 And the Lord plagued Pharaoh and his house with great plagues because of Sarai Abram's wife. 18 And Pharaoh called Abram and said, What is this that thou hast done unto me? why didst thou not tell me that she was thy wife? 19 Why*

saidst thou, She is my sister? so I might have taken her to me to wife: now therefore behold thy wife, take her, and go thy way.

However, we see that the wealth came in after Abraham left Egypt. We see this In Genesis Chapter 13 from verse 1 to 4.

Principle Two – Relationship and Prophecy

Genesis 30: 27, *"And Laban said unto him, I pray thee, if I have found favour in thine eyes, tarry: for I have learned by experience that the Lord hath blessed me for thy sake."*

Abraham's blessing extended to his nephew Lot, despite the promise not being directly made to him, illustrating that when God blesses His chosen, He also blesses those connected to them. This principle is further exemplified in the story of Jacob and Laban in Genesis 30:27, where Laban acknowledges that he has experienced blessings because of his relationship with Jacob.

This first principle leads us to the next principle of wealth, which emphasizes the importance of having a relationship with individuals who possess divine instruction and prophetic guidance. Throughout the Bible, we find instances where people attained wealth through their association with those whom God had called to prosperity. As mentioned earlier, Lot experienced abundance through his connection with Abraham, as discussed in the previous principle. Similarly, Laban also benefited from his relationship with Jacob, as previously mentioned.

We see a similar story between Potiphar and Joseph in Genesis 39:5 and it says: ***"From the time he put him in charge of his household and of all that he owned; the LORD blessed the household of the Egyptian because of Joseph. The blessing of the LORD was on everything***

Potiphar had, both in the house and in the field."

This verse confirms that God blessed Potiphar's household and all his possessions because of Joseph's presence and the responsibility he was given.

Another example is the story of one of the wives of the sons of the prophet whose creditors were out to take her sons before she cried out to the prophet for help. This story you would find in 2 Kings 4:1-7. According to the story, the wife of one of the sons of the prophet Elisha died, leaving her husband in debt. As creditors were coming to take her two sons as slaves to pay off the debt, she sought help from Elisha.

An important lesson to learn from this story is that it is possible to be close to the source of wealth and not have it and worst still is even die and not have a taste of it. This son of the Prophet did not understand this principle early enough until he died but the wife cashed in on it and lived in abundance for the rest of her life. The tragedy of the story was not just that he died a poor man and a burden with debt for his family, the account also suggests that he was a godly man, he feared the Lord which meant he was a righteous man. In fact, as one of the sons of the Prophet, he was training to become a prophet. This testimony is from his own wife in verse 1 of that chapter "Now there cried a certain woman of the wives of the sons of the prophets unto Elisha, saying, Thy servant my husband is dead; and thou knowest that thy servant did fear the Lord: and the creditor is come to take unto him my two sons to be bondmen."

This same description was used to describe Lot in 2 Peter 2:7-8. Even though both men were righteous, that did not mean they had the grace for prosperity. They needed to be properly aligned.

This relationship principle is also closely related to the prophecy from the man God has graced with the grace of prosperity. The creative power of prophecy works can create what did not exist before now and bring it to life. An example is what we see in the story in 2 Kings 7:1-20.

In the story, during a time of famine in the city of Samaria, the prophet Elisha foretold that food supplies would become abundant and affordable overnight. The royal officer, who served as the king's right-hand man, expressed doubt about Elisha's prophecy, questioning how such a thing could happen.

Elisha responded by declaring that the officer would witness the fulfillment of the prophecy but would not partake in the benefits. Four lepers, who were outcasts living on the outskirts of the city, discovered that the enemy camp outside the city had been deserted. They went and reported this to the gatekeepers of Samaria, and the news quickly reached the king and his officer.

The starving people of Samaria rushed out to the enemy camp, finding it filled with abundant food and supplies, just as Elisha had prophesied. The royal officer, however, did not live to enjoy the benefits. As the starving people trampled each other in their haste to obtain the provisions, the officer was stationed at the gate and was crushed to death.

Another example you will find in Ezra 6 verse 14 *"And the elders of the Jews builded, and they prospered through the prophesying of Haggai the prophet and Zechariah the son of Iddo. And they builded, and finished it, according to the commandment of the God of Israel, and according to the commandment of Cyrus, and Darius, and Artaxerxes king of Persia."*

This principle is summarized in 2 Chronicles 20 verse 20, *"And they rose early in the morning, and went forth into the wilderness of Tekoa: and as they went forth, Jehoshaphat stood and said, Hear me, O Judah, and ye inhabitants of Jerusalem; Believe in the Lord your God, so shall ye be established; believe his prophets, so shall ye prosper."*

This second principle, though equally efficient as the first, is not automatic. There are other considerations to keep in mind for it to work and that is the rule of service.

In the account of Genesis 13, Lot would have perpetually been blessed if he understood this principle. The rule of relationship is littered all over the Bible. Lot failed to acknowledge the source of his wealth. He assumed that because he had become blessed like Abraham, he did not need him anymore. To maintain the wealth from this source, one must remain attached to this physical person that God has used to bring them wealth. This attachment or connection does not have to be physical, however, it must be clear and evident from their relationship and behaviour for this person to acknowledge where they received their wealth from.

This principle is not only in relation to wealth creation but also in relation achieving one's God given assignment. We see this evidence in the story of Elijah and Elisha. First in 1 Kings 19:19-21, and then 2 Kings 2:1-15

1 Kings 19:19-21

"19 So he departed thence, and found Elisha the son of Shaphat, who was plowing with twelve yoke of oxen before him, and he with the twelfth: and Elijah passed by him, and cast his mantle upon him. 20 And he left the oxen, and ran after Elijah, and said, Let me, I pray thee, kiss my father and my mother, and then I will follow thee. And he said unto him, Go back again: for what have I done to thee? 21 And he returned back from him, and took a yoke of oxen, and slew them, and

boiled their flesh with the instruments of the oxen, and gave unto the people, and they did eat. Then he arose, and went after Elijah, and ministered unto him."

2 Kings 2:1-15

"2 And it came to pass, when the Lord would take up Elijah into heaven by a whirlwind, that Elijah went with Elisha from Gilgal. 2 And Elijah said unto Elisha, Tarry here, I pray thee; for the Lord hath sent me to Bethel. And Elisha said unto him, As the Lord liveth, and as thy soul liveth, I will not leave thee. So they went down to Bethel. 3 And the sons of the prophets that were at Bethel came forth to Elisha, and said unto him, Knowest thou that the Lord

will take away thy master from thy head to day? And he said, Yea, I know it; hold ye your peace. 4 And Elijah said unto him, Elisha, tarry here, I pray thee; for the Lord hath sent me to Jericho. And he said, As the Lord liveth, and as thy soul liveth, I will not leave thee. So, they came to Jericho. 5 And the sons of the prophets that were at Jericho came to Elisha, and said unto him, Knowest thou that the Lord will take away thy master from thy head to day? And he answered, Yea, I know it; hold ye your peace. 6 And Elijah said unto him, Tarry, I pray thee, here; for the Lord hath sent me to Jordan. And he said, As the Lord liveth, and as thy soul liveth, I will not leave thee. And they two went on. 7 And fifty men of the sons of the prophets went, and stood to view afar off: and they two stood by Jordan. 8 And Elijah took his mantle, and wrapped it together, and smote the waters, and they were divided hither and thither, so that they two went over on dry ground. 9 And it came to pass, when they were gone over, that Elijah said unto Elisha, Ask what I shall do for thee, before I be taken away from thee. And Elisha said, I pray thee, let a double portion of thy spirit be upon me. 10 And he said, Thou hast asked a hard thing: nevertheless, if thou see me when I am taken from thee, it shall be so unto thee; but if not, it shall not be so. 11 And it came to pass, as they still went on, and talked, that, behold, there appeared a chariot of fire, and horses of fire, and parted them both asunder; and Elijah went up by a whirlwind into heaven. 12 And Elisha saw it, and he cried, My father, my father, the chariot of Israel, and the horsemen thereof. And he saw him no more: and he took hold of his own clothes, and rent them in two pieces. 13 He took up also the mantle of Elijah that fell from him, and went back, and stood by the bank of Jordan; 14 And he took the mantle of Elijah that fell from him, and smote the waters, and said, Where is the Lord God of Elijah? and when he also had smitten the waters, they parted hither and thither: and Elisha went over. 15 And when the sons of the prophets which were to view at Jericho saw him, they said, The spirit of Elijah doth rest on Elisha. And they came to meet him, and bowed themselves to the ground before him."

The story of Elijah and Elisha carries several lessons and principles that can be gleaned from their interactions and experiences. This story demonstrates many qualities expected from one who expects to receive the reward from another. Among them are obedience, surrender to authority, service, loyalty, teachability, faithfulness, perseverance, honour, respect and of course humility.

Even when others mocked Elisha, he remained resolute to the course and eventually he received the reward. In the scheme of things Elisha was not supposed to be the next prophet after Elijah, the next prophet should ideally come from the school of the prophets, he was a farmer or a plower of the land, however, he positioned himself carefully for the blessing to drop on him. Here are a few lessons that can be drawn from their story:

- Obedience and Surrender: Elisha's immediate response to Elijah's call and his willingness to leave his occupation and follow him exemplify obedience and surrender. It teaches us the importance of being open and receptive to God's calling in our lives, even if it means leaving behind familiar or comfortable circumstances.

- Discipleship and Mentorship: Elisha's journey with Elijah represents the concept of discipleship and mentorship. Elisha learned from Elijah, served him faithfully, and sought to inherit his spiritual legacy.

- Faithfulness and Perseverance: Elisha's determination to stay with Elijah, even when asked to remain behind, demonstrates faithfulness and perseverance. It teaches us the importance of remaining committed to our calling, even in the face of challenges, distractions, or discouragement.

- God's Power and Provision: The miracles and supernatural acts performed through Elijah and Elisha display the power and provision of God. From parting the waters of the Jordan River to multiplying oil, raising the dead, and more, these miracles remind us of God's ability to intervene in extraordinary ways and provide for His people.

- Passing the Mantle: The symbolic act of Elijah passing his mantle to Elisha signifies the passing of spiritual authority and responsibility from one generation to the next.

- Desire for God's Presence: Elisha's request for a double portion of Elijah's spirit reveals his hunger for a deeper experience of God's presence and power.

- Honor and Respect: Elisha's reverence and honor for Elijah are evident throughout their interactions. It underscores the significance of respecting spiritual leaders, mentors, and elders in our lives and valuing the wisdom and guidance they offer.

These are just a few of the lessons that can be gleaned from the story of Elijah and Elisha. Individuals may find additional insights and applications based on their own reflections and spiritual journey.

Other examples of this principle are.

- Moses and Joshua (Numbers 27:18-23, Deuteronomy 31:1-8): Moses was the great leader of the Israelites, and Joshua served as his assistant and apprentice. Moses appointed Joshua as his successor, and Joshua learned from Moses, eventually leading the Israelites into the Promised Land.

- Paul and Timothy (Acts 16:1-3, 2 Timothy 1:2-5): Paul, the apostle, mentored and discipled Timothy, a young disciple and fellow worker in ministry. Paul entrusted Timothy with important responsibilities and encouraged him to grow in his faith and leadership.

- Eli and Samuel (1 Samuel 3:1-21): Eli, a priest and judge, served as a mentor to the young Samuel. Eli provided guidance and spiritual instruction to Samuel, who eventually became a prophet and one of Israel's greatest leaders.

- Naomi and Ruth (Ruth 1:1-22, Ruth 2:1-23): Naomi, Ruth's mother-in-law, guided and mentored Ruth as she navigated challenging circumstances. Naomi provided wisdom and guidance, leading Ruth to eventually find a new husband and become part of the lineage of King David.

- Mordecai and Esther (Esther 2:5-7, Esther 4:12-17): Mordecai, Esther's cousin, served as a mentor and guide to her. He encouraged her to embrace her identity and take courageous action to save the Jewish people.

Adhering to this fundamental principle can yield success, while deviating from it carries consequences. This truth is exemplified by the tragic fate of Lot's wife in Genesis 19:26, where her disobedience resulted in her untimely demise. Likewise, had Lot's relationship with Abraham not been strained, he may not have found himself compelled to leave Sodom and Gomorrah. Another illustration of the principle is found in the account of Elisha's servant, Gehazi, who suffered the affliction of leprosy as chronicled in 2 Kings 5:27. Furthermore, in 2 Kings 7:2, we encounter the narrative of the royal officer, a trusted aide to the king, underscoring the importance of adhering to this principle for favorable outcomes.

Principle Three - The Wisdom Principle

The third principle to lasting wealth creation we shall be discussing here is wisdom. In the conventional definition of wisdom, it is believed that it is the application of knowledge. While this definition may be right in a sense, it is not a complete definition. Wisdom, according to the Bible, refers to a deep understanding and practical knowledge that comes from a reverent fear and relationship with God. It encompasses insight, discernment, and the ability to apply knowledge to make wise choices and live in alignment with God's principles. Wisdom is not merely intellectual knowledge or cleverness but a spiritual and moral understanding that leads to righteous living.

Here are a few key aspects of wisdom as described in the Bible:

- Fear of the Lord: Proverbs 9:10 states, *"The fear of the LORD is the beginning of wisdom, and knowledge of the Holy One is understanding."* Wisdom starts with a proper reverence and awe for God, recognizing His sovereignty, holiness, and authority. It involves acknowledging God's wisdom and seeking to align one's life with His ways.

- Instruction and Teaching: Wisdom is acquired through seeking, receiving instruction, and teaching. Proverbs 4:7 advises, *"The beginning of wisdom is this: Get wisdom. Though it cost all you have, get understanding."* This emphasizes the active pursuit of wisdom through studying and meditating on God's Word, seeking guidance from godly mentors, and being open to correction and instruction.

- Discernment and Understanding: Wisdom involves discernment, the ability to perceive truth and make sound judgments. Proverbs 3:13-14 says, "**Blessed are those who find wisdom, those who gain understanding, for she is more profitable than silver and yields better returns than gold**." It emphasizes the value of discernment and understanding, which lead to making wise decisions and living a blessed life.

- Application and Righteous Living: Wisdom is not just theoretical knowledge but is demonstrated through practical application. James

3:13 states, "*Who is wise and understanding among you? Let them show it by their good life, by deeds done in the humility that comes from wisdom.*" True wisdom is reflected in righteous behaviour, humility, and a consistent adherence to God's commandments and principles.

- God's Gift and Christ as the Wisdom of God: Wisdom is ultimately a gift from God. In 1 Corinthians 1:24, it is said that Jesus Christ is "*the power of God and the wisdom of God.*" Christ embodies wisdom, and through a relationship with Him, believers can grow in wisdom and understanding.

In relation to building lasting wealth, wisdom is personified in Proverbs 8:18-21, and this is what wisdom is saying of herself.

18 Riches and honour are with me; yea, durable riches and righteousness. 19 My fruit is better than gold, yea, than fine gold; and my revenue than choice silver. 20 I lead in the way of righteousness, in the midst of the paths of judgment: 21 That I may cause those that love me to inherit substance; and I will fill their treasures.

Following from the above, we can see all the different shades of wisdom. Let us now delve into more practical application of building lasting wealth through wisdom by acquiring looking some of the elements. We will be drawn from the book of James 3: 17, ***But the wisdom that is from above is first pure, then peaceable, gentle, and easy to be intreated, full of mercy and good fruits, without partiality, and without hypocrisy.***

The above passage gives a summary of the eight elements of wisdom that we will discuss in the next chapter.

CHAPTER FOUR

THE EIGHT ELEMENTS OF WISDOM

CHAPTER FOUR

THE EIGHT ELEMENTS OF WISDOM

The eight elements of wisdom are the subject of James 3: 17, **"But the wisdom that is from above is first pure, then peaceable, gentle, and easy to be intreated, full of mercy and good fruits, without partiality, and without hypocrisy."**

First Element – Purity

This is what we highlighted in the previous chapter earlier in Proverbs 9:10 which states that, **"The fear of the LORD is the beginning of wisdom, and knowledge of the Holy One is understanding."** It is the fear of God that intreat us to purity. Do not be deceived, the rules have not changed. There are no other rules to it and God does not adjust this rule per person. It is applicable to everyone He calls. In Hebrews 12 verse 14 it says, "*Make every effort to live in peace with everyone and to be holy; without holiness no one will see the Lord.*" The emphases here is the second sentence, "*...without holiness no one will see the Lord.*".

Purity as a state of moral and spiritual cleanliness, free from contamination, impurity, or defilement. It encompasses various aspects of a person's life, thoughts, and actions. Here are some key elements of purity according to the Bible:

- **Moral Integrity**: Purity involves living with moral integrity, adhering to God's standards of righteousness and avoiding sinful behavior. It includes being honest, truthful, and having a sincere heart before God and others. See Proverbs 11:3 and Psalm 15:2.

- **Sexual Purity**: The Bible places a strong emphasis on sexual purity, which involves reserving sexual activity for the context of marriage between a husband and wife. It encourages abstinence before marriage and faithfulness within marriage, while rejecting sexual immorality and impure desires. There have been many debates about sexual purity of late with many perversions including endorsement from those who are supposed to be custodians of the truth, from so-called preachers. The secret to knowing if you are deviating from the word of God and violating sexual purity is when you begin to rationalize and justify an act or debate what is clear in the Bible to know whether it applies to a section of the people or whether Jesus' death has exempted you from it. There is no exemption from sexual purity. In fact, in relation to sexual purity, the creation has it tougher, in Matthew 5:28 this is Jesus' own take on the issue *"But I tell you that anyone who looks at a woman to lust after her has already committed adultery with her in his heart."* See also in 1 Corinthians 6 verse 18 - 20 and Hebrews 13 verse 4.

Mighty men (including women) fall into the sin of sexual impurity because they got too comfortable with their idea that they may now be immune or the illusion that they have become too strong to fall for this obvious sin. Many mighty men through time have become victim of this sin. It is likely that you know someone who is a victim.

A particularly good example is Samson in Judges 16:4-22. This passage recounts the account of Samson's relationship with Delilah, who was approached by the Philistines to discover the secret of Samson's strength. Delilah persistently seeks to learn the source of his strength and eventually succeeds in persuading Samson to reveal that his strength lies in his hair. Delilah then betrays Samson by cutting off his hair while he sleeps, leading to his capture and subsequent loss of his strength. This is the same strategy of the devil, the same tactics, the same scheme. If you ever find yourself in this corridor, run! This is what it says in 1 Corinthians 6 verse 18, *"Flee fornication...".* You will never win if you hesitate.

- **Pure Thoughts and Intentions**: Purity extends to the realm of thoughts and intentions. It involves guarding the mind against impure thoughts, lustful desires, and wicked intentions. Philippians 4:8 instructs believers to focus on things that are true, honorable, just, pure, lovely, commendable, excellent, and praiseworthy.

- **Heart Purity**: Purity is a matter of the heart. Jesus teaches in Matthew 5:8, *"Blessed are the pure in heart, for they shall see God."* A pure heart involves having right motives, a genuine love for God, and a sincere devotion to Him. See also Psalm 51:10.

- **Spiritual Cleansing**: Purity is also associated with spiritual cleansing. It involves confessing sins, repenting, and seeking forgiveness from God. 1 John 1 verse 9 assures believers that if they confess their sins, God is faithful and just to forgive and cleanse them from all unrighteousness. See also James 4 verse 8.

- **Separation from Worldly Influence**: Purity may involve separating oneself from worldly influences and avoiding association with sinful practices or people who may lead one astray. It includes pursuing a life that is set apart for God's purposes and dedicated to His service. See 2 Corinthians 6 verse 17, Psalm 1 verse 1 and Romans 12 verse 2.

If your plan is to build lasting wealth, purity should be your number one watchword. In the Bible it encompasses a holistic and integrated approach to living a righteous and blameless life before God and others. It involves aligning one's thoughts, words, actions, and motivations with God's standards of holiness and seeking His help to maintain a pure and undefiled heart. If this feels overwhelming or impossible, you are not asking the Holy Spirit for strength and you do not want God's help because in 2 Corinthians 12 verse 9, "***And he said unto me, My grace is sufficient for thee: for my strength is made perfect in weakness...***"

Second Element - Peaceable

This is the second element of wisdom according to James 3 verse 17. There are many references to peace and being peaceable in the bible. The word "peaceable" in the Bible is derived from the Greek term "eirēnikos," which is used to describe a person or attitude that promotes peace and harmony. In the context of biblical teachings, being peaceable involves actively pursuing peace, seeking reconciliation, and fostering unity among individuals and communities.

Here are a few key aspects of what it means to be peaceable according to the Bible:

- **Pursuing Peace**: Being peaceable means actively striving for peace in relationships and interactions. This includes avoiding conflict, promoting understanding, and seeking to resolve disagreements in a peaceful manner. Romans 12:18.

- **Reconciliation**: Being peaceable involves a commitment to reconciliation. This includes seeking to restore broken relationships and working towards healing and forgiveness. It emphasizes the importance of pursuing peace even in the face of differences or past conflicts. James 3:18.

  This also involves reconciling others who are separated from God to God. This is found in 2 Corinthians 5:18. The verse states: "*All this is from God, who reconciled us to himself through Christ and gave us the ministry of reconciliation.*" This verse highlights that God, through Christ, has reconciled believers to Himself, bridging the gap between humanity and God. As a result, believers are entrusted with the ministry of reconciliation. This ministry involves sharing the message of reconciliation and inviting others to be reconciled to God through faith in Jesus Christ. The following verses in 2 Corinthians 5:19-20 further explain this ministry: "*that God was reconciling the world to himself in Christ, not counting people's sins against them. And he has committed to us the message of reconciliation. We are therefore Christ's ambassadors, as though God were making his appeal through us. We implore you on Christ's behalf: Be reconciled to God.*" These verses emphasize that believers are ambassadors for Christ, serving as representatives of God's reconciling work in the world. It is a calling to proclaim the Gospel, share God's love, and invite others to enter into a restored relationship with Him. This is also confirmed in Proverbs 11:30 that "*The fruit of the righteous is a tree of life, and he who wins souls is wise.*"

- **Peacemakers**: Jesus teaches in Matthew 5:9, "*Blessed are the peacemakers, for they will be called children of God.*" Being peaceable means actively working to bring about peace and harmony in one's own life and in the world. It involves being a bridge-builder, promoting understanding, and seeking peaceful resolutions.

- **Unity and Harmony**: Being peaceable entails promoting unity and harmony among believers and within the community. It involves cultivating an atmosphere of love, compassion, and mutual respect, fostering an environment where relationships can thrive. Proverbs 12:20.

- **Resisting Strife and Conflict**: Being peaceable also means resisting the temptation to engage in strife, quarrels, or divisive behaviour. It encourages avoiding actions, words, or attitudes that can disrupt peace and harm relationships. 1 Peter 3:11.

Being peaceable according to the Bible involves actively pursuing peace, seeking reconciliation, promoting unity, and resisting actions or attitudes that disrupt harmony. It is a mindset and lifestyle that reflects the character of Christ and contributes to a peaceful and loving community.

Third Element – Gentle

The word "gentle" as used in the Bible refers to a specific character trait that involves meekness, humility, and a gentle spirit in one's interactions with others. It is often associated with being considerate, patient, and kind. Here are a few Bible references that shed light on the meaning of "gentle":

- Matthew 11:29 (NIV): "*Take my yoke upon you and learn from me, for I am gentle and humble in heart, and you will find rest for your souls.*" In this verse, Jesus describes Himself as gentle and humble, inviting others to learn from His example.

- Galatians 5:22-23 (NIV): "*But the fruit of the Spirit is love, joy, peace, forbearance, kindness, goodness, faithfulness, gentleness and self-*

control. Against such things there is no law." This passage lists the fruits of the Spirit, which include gentleness. It highlights how gentleness is a quality that is produced by the Holy Spirit in the lives of believers.

- Ephesians 4:2 (NIV): "*Be completely humble and gentle; be patient, bearing with one another in love.*" Here, believers are urged to demonstrate humility, gentleness, patience, and love in their interactions with others.

- Colossians 3:12 (NIV): "*Therefore, as God's chosen people, holy and dearly loved, clothe yourselves with compassion, kindness, humility, gentleness and patience.*" This verse encourages believers to put on gentleness as part of their new identity in Christ, along with other virtues.

- 1 Peter 3:15 (NIV): "*But in your hearts revere Christ as Lord. Always be prepared to give an answer to everyone who asks you to give the reason for the hope that you have. But do this with gentleness and respect.*" This verse emphasizes the importance of presenting the message of hope with gentleness and respect, even when faced with questions or challenges.

These Bible references depict gentleness as a virtue that believers are encouraged to embody in their attitudes, words, and actions. It involves having a gentle and humble disposition, treating others with kindness and respect, and reflecting the character of Christ.

Fourth Element – Easy to be intreated.

The phrase "easy to be intreated" is found in James 3:17 in the King James Version of the Bible. However, it is important to note that the term "easy to be intreated" is somewhat archaic and may be better understood in modern language as "willing to yield" or "open to reason."

In James 3 verse 17, it says *"But the wisdom that is from above is first pure, then peaceable, gentle, and easy to be intreated, full of mercy and good fruits, without partiality, and without hypocrisy."*

Here, James is describing the characteristics of godly wisdom. "Easy to be intreated" suggests a willingness to listen, understand, and be open to reason or persuasion. It implies a humble and teachable spirit that is receptive to the viewpoints and needs of others. It reflects an attitude of humility and a willingness to consider different perspectives in pursuit of peace and righteousness. An understanding that one's opinion may not be valid or right.

The concept of being "easy to be intreated" aligns with the broader biblical teachings on humility, love, and the importance of considering others' needs. It encourages believers to approach discussions, conflicts, and interactions with a gentle and open-hearted attitude, seeking understanding and unity rather than stubbornness or an unyielding spirit.

Fifth Element - Full of Mercy

Being full of mercy is a characteristic that is not negotiable. This is because we also have received mercy to be where we are today.

The mercy of God saved us, and it is intended that we extend the hand of mercy to others.

The phrase "full of mercy" refers to the attribute of showing compassion, kindness, and forgiveness towards others, particularly in their time of need or when they have committed wrong. In the Bible, it is used to describe the merciful nature of God and the behavior expected of believers in their interactions with others.

There are many examples in the bible that depicts the need to be merciful. The parable of the unmerciful servant is found in Matthew 18:21-35 in the Bible. It is commonly known as the Parable of the Unforgiving Servant. Here is a summary of the parable:

The parable begins with Peter asking Jesus how many times he should forgive someone who sins against him. Jesus responds by telling a story about a king who wanted to settle accounts with his servants. One servant owed him an enormous debt that he could not repay—ten thousand talents, an astronomical sum.

Since the servant could not repay, the king ordered him and his family to be sold as slaves to recover some of the debt. However, the servant pleaded with the king, asking for patience and promising to repay everything. In response, the king had compassion on the servant and forgave him for the entire debt, releasing him.

After being forgiven, the servant encountered another fellow servant who owed him a much smaller amount—only a hundred denarii. Despite having been forgiven such a significant debt himself, the servant grabbed his fellow servant and demanded payment. When the fellow servant begged for mercy, the unforgiving servant refused and had him thrown into prison until the debt was paid.

Other servants witnessed this and reported it to the king. The king summoned the unforgiving servant and confronted him, saying that he should have shown the same mercy he received. The king was angry and handed the servant over to be tortured until he could repay the original debt, highlighting the severe consequences of his lack of forgiveness.

The parable concludes with Jesus stating, *"So also my heavenly Father will do to every one of you if you do not forgive your brother from your heart"* (Matthew 18:35, ESV). This emphasizes the importance of forgiveness and warns against harboring unforgiveness in our hearts.

The parable teaches the principle of forgiveness, emphasizing the immense mercy God extends to us by forgiving our sins. It highlights that since we have been forgiven much, we should also extend forgiveness to others. Failure to do so will result in consequences and hinder our relationship with God.

Here are a few Bible references that highlight the concept of being "full of mercy":

- Matthew 5:7 (NIV): "**Blessed are the merciful, for they will be shown mercy.**" In the Beatitudes, Jesus teaches that those who show mercy to others will receive mercy themselves.

- Luke 6:36 (NIV): "**Be merciful, just as your Father is merciful.**" Jesus instructs His followers to demonstrate the same mercy and compassion that God shows to them.

- James 2:13 (NIV): **"Because judgment without mercy will be shown to anyone who has not been merciful. Mercy triumphs over judgment."** This verse emphasizes the importance of showing mercy to others, as mercy will prevail over harsh judgment.

- Micah 6:8 (NIV): **"He has shown you, O mortal, what is good. And what does the LORD require of you? To act justly and to love mercy and to walk humbly with your God."** This verse highlights the significance of loving mercy as one of the requirements of a faithful relationship with God.

- Ephesians 2:4 (NIV): "*But because of his great love for us, God, who is rich in mercy...*" This verse highlights the abundant and generous nature of God's mercy towards humanity.

Sixth Element - Good Fruits

In the Bible, the term "good fruits" refers to the righteous actions, attitudes, and behaviours that are produced in the lives of believers who are walking in obedience to God and filled with the Holy Spirit. Good fruits are the outward evidence of a transformed heart and a genuine relationship with God. Good fruits results from constant communion with the Holy Spirit, the word of God and fellowship with the brethren. Our interactions with these three components mentioned will show in our character and behaviours towards God and others.

Here are some Bible references that highlight the concept of good fruits:

- Matthew 7:16-20: In this passage, Jesus teaches about discerning true prophets by their fruits. He states that a good tree (representing a person with a genuine relationship with God) bears good fruits, while a bad tree (representing a person who is false or lacking a genuine relationship with God) bears bad fruits.

- Galatians 5:22-23: The Apostle Paul describes the fruits of the Spirit in this passage. He lists love, joy, peace, patience, kindness, goodness, faithfulness, gentleness, and self-control as the manifestations of the Holy Spirit's work in the life of a believer.

- Ephesians 5:9: Paul urges believers to "walk as children of light" and explains that the fruit of light consists of all that is good, right, and true.

- Colossians 1:10: Paul prays that the Colossian believers may "walk in a manner worthy of the Lord, fully pleasing to him, bearing fruit in every good work."

- James 3:17-18: James describes the wisdom that comes from above, stating that it is "pure, then peaceable, gentle, open to reason, full of mercy and good fruits, impartial and sincere." This passage connects good fruits with godly wisdom and righteous living.

The verses mentioned emphasize that good fruits encompass a broad spectrum of positive attitudes, actions, and virtues that mirror God's character and the transformative work of the Holy Spirit in the life of a believer. These fruits include love, joy, peace, kindness, patience, faithfulness, self-control, and other righteous behaviors that vividly demonstrate a life transformed by Christ.

As followers of Christ, it is crucial that our identity shines clearly, revealing our Christ-like nature. When our character lacks these qualities, our witness becomes blurred, hindering the display of good fruit and the application of wisdom in our lives.

Seventh Element - Without partiality

The phrase "without partiality" refers to being unbiased, fair, and treating people equally, without showing favouritism or discrimination based on external factors such as social status, wealth, or appearance. It implies impartiality and treating all individuals with equity and justice. In the Bible, this concept is often associated with God's character and His expectation for His people to display similar impartiality in their interactions.

Examples can be found in the life and ministry of Jesus Christ. Throughout the Gospels, Jesus consistently demonstrated impartiality in His interactions with people. He reached out to individuals from various walks of life, including the poor, the marginalized, the sick, and even those considered social outcasts. Jesus did not show favouritism based on social status, ethnicity, or any other external factors. Here are a few examples of Jesus displaying impartiality:

- Jesus and the Samaritan Woman (John 4:1-42): In this encounter, Jesus engaged in conversation with a Samaritan woman at a well. This was significant because Jews and Samaritans had a history of hostility and were divided along religious and ethnic lines. Yet, Jesus treated the woman with respect, addressed her spiritual needs, and revealed Himself as the Messiah to her.

- Jesus and the Roman Centurion (Matthew 8:5-13): A Roman centurion, a Gentile and an officer of the occupying Roman army, approached Jesus seeking healing for his servant.

Jesus commended the centurion's faith and granted his request, demonstrating His impartiality and willingness to help people regardless of their background.

- Jesus and Zacchaeus (Luke 19:1-10): Zacchaeus, a tax collector and considered a sinner by society, climbed a tree to see Jesus. Despite the social stigma associated with Zacchaeus' occupation and reputation, Jesus showed impartiality by choosing to dine with him and extending salvation to him and his household.

Here are a few Bible passages that illustrate the importance of being impartial:

- Acts 10:34-35: **"*Then Peter began to speak: 'I now realize how true it is that God does not show favoritism*** *but accepts from every nation the one who fears him and does what is right.*'" This verse underscores God's impartiality and His acceptance of people from all nations who have a reverent fear of Him and live in righteousness.

- Romans 2:11: "*For God does not show favoritism.*" This verse emphasizes God's impartiality, affirming that He treats all people equally, without any bias or partiality.

- James 2:1-4: "*My brothers and sisters, believers in our glorious Lord Jesus Christ must not show favoritism. Suppose a man comes into your meeting wearing a gold ring and fine clothes, and a poor man in filthy old clothes also comes in. If you show special attention to the man wearing fine clothes and say, 'Here's a good seat for you,' but say to the poor man, 'You stand there' or 'Sit on the floor by my feet,' have you not discriminated among yourselves and become judges with evil thoughts?"* This passage admonishes believers to avoid favouritism and partiality, specifically addressing the issue of treating the rich more favorably than the poor.

- 1 Peter 1:17: "*Since you call on a Father who judges each person's work impartially, live out your time as foreigners here in reverent fear*." This verse reminds believers that God, as a just and impartial Judge, evaluates each person's work without any bias. It encourages them to live their lives in a manner that reflects a reverent fear of God.

These verses emphasize the significance of treating all people with fairness and equality, just as God does. God is impartial, meaning that he does not show favoritism to anyone. He loves and accepts all people, regardless of their race, ethnicity, social status, or any other superficial factor.

Believers are called to imitate God's impartiality in their attitudes, actions, and treatment of others. This means that we should not judge others based on their appearance, their background, or their circumstances. Instead, we should treat everyone with respect and dignity, regardless of who they are or what they have done.

When we imitate God's impartiality, we are showing that we are following his example and that we are living according to his will. We are also helping to create a more just and equitable world.

Here are some specific ways that we can imitate God's impartiality:

- We can be mindful of our words and our actions, and we can avoid making any discriminatory statements or gestures.
- We can be fair and just in our dealings with others, regardless of their social status or economic background.
- We can stand up for those who are being treated unfairly, and we can speak out against injustice.
- We can work to create a more inclusive and welcoming environment for

everyone, regardless of their differences.

It is not always easy to imitate God's impartiality, but it is important. When we do, we are showing that we are following God's example and that we are treating others with the respect and dignity that they deserve.

Eighth element - Without hypocrisy

The phrase "without hypocrisy" means to be genuine, sincere, and free from deceit or pretense. In the biblical context, it refers to a character trait that is honest, transparent, and authentic in one's words, actions, and motives.

Being without hypocrisy is especially crucial in our service within the house of God. If you are actively engaged in building the church through your service, do so with a sincere heart, avoiding the temptation to merely perform for others' approval or seek personal recognition. Here are several Bible references that emphasize the significance of authenticity and genuineness:

- Romans 12:9: *"Let love be without hypocrisy. Abhor what is evil. Cling to what is good."* This verse encourages believers to love genuinely and without pretense, detesting evil and holding fast to what is good.
- 1 Peter 1:22: *"Since you have purified your souls in obeying the truth through the Spirit in sincere love of the brethren, love one another fervently with a pure heart."* This verse urges believers to have sincere love for one another,

emphasizing the importance of genuine affection and purity of heart.

- James 3:17: "**But the wisdom that is from above is first pure, then peaceable, gentle, willing to yield, full of mercy and good fruits, without partiality and without hypocrisy.**" This verse describes the characteristics of godly wisdom, emphasizing that it is free from hypocrisy among other qualities.

- Matthew 23:28: "**Even so you also outwardly appear righteous to men, but inside you are full of hypocrisy and lawlessness.**" In this verse, Jesus rebukes the Pharisees for their outward show of righteousness while lacking sincerity and genuine obedience to God's laws.

These passages, along with many others, underscore the biblical standard for believers to embrace integrity, sincerity, and honesty. They emphasize the importance of living with authenticity and genuine devotion to God, not only in our relationships with others but also in our personal commitment to Him. Being without hypocrisy entails aligning our words, actions, and attitudes in a manner that genuinely reflects our unwavering dedication to God's truth and love. It calls us to embody a consistent and sincere faith, demonstrating integrity in every aspect of our lives.

In conclusion James 3:17, the verse describes the eight elements of wisdom that are from above:

- **Purity**: Wisdom from above is characterized by a foundation of moral purity and righteousness.

- **Peaceable**: It promotes peace, harmony, and reconciliation among people.

- **Gentle**: Wisdom demonstrates a gentle and considerate attitude towards others, showing kindness and compassion.

- **Willing to yield**: It is open to reason and willing to listen, value others' perspectives, and consider alternative viewpoints.

- **Full of mercy**: Wisdom is marked by a compassionate and forgiving nature, extending mercy and grace to others.

- **Good fruits**: It produces good deeds and bears the fruit of righteousness in one's life.

- **Without partiality**: Wisdom is impartial and unbiased, treating all people fairly and without favoritism.
- **Without hypocrisy**: It is genuine, sincere, and free from deceit or pretense, aligning words and actions consistently.

The elements of wisdom listed in James 3:17 can indeed be seen as character traits that contribute to both spiritual and material wealth. When individuals embody purity, peaceability, gentleness, and other qualities of wisdom, it can positively impact their relationships, decision-making, and actions related to wealth creation. By valuing wisdom and pursuing it above material riches, as highlighted in Proverbs 8:10-11, individuals prioritize the acquisition and application of wisdom, which can lead to both spiritual and material prosperity.

CHAPTER FIVE

THE VEHICLES FOR WEALTH CREATION

CHAPTER FIVE
THE VEHICLES FOR WEALTH CREATION

Based on the aforementioned principles, it is crucial to recognize that there are two primary avenues that God has provided for creating wealth. All the principles we have discussed find their expression through these two channels, whether acquired through obedience to God, through relationships, or by means of prophecy and application of wisdom.

It is worth noting that we have not specifically mentioned wealth obtained through inheritance. This omission is intentional because even individuals who inherit wealth must understand that they are still expected to utilize the vehicles suggested in the Bible to preserve and make their wealth enduring.

Inheritance alone does not guarantee prosperity; it is through the application of biblical principles that wealth can be wisely managed and made lasting. There are instances where individuals have acquired wealth through inheritance, only to squander it on frivolous and unsustainable lifestyles. This can occur when they disregard or are not adequately educated about the proper utilization of these avenues we are about to discuss. It serves as a reminder that simply receiving an inheritance does not automatically ensure wise stewardship or long-term prosperity. Understanding and implementing the biblical principles associated with wealth management and the appropriate channels for its preservation are essential for making wise and sustainable choices, regardless of how wealth is obtained.

These vehicles are for wealth built through employment and wealth built through business. We will be discussing how wealth can be built using these two vehicles.

Building Wealth Through Employment

In the Bible, we find examples of individuals who built wealth through their employment, such as Joseph, Daniel, and Jacob. Joseph and Daniel served in the public sector or government, while Jacob initially worked for a one-man business before eventually establishing his own business.

In Genesis 41:37-44, we read how Joseph ended up as wealthy man. But this is not where the story began. Joseph possessed a unique gift, but it was honed through the various events he experienced. This story holds particular relevance today, as many people face circumstances beyond their control. Joseph's life exemplifies the ability to overcome unimaginable challenges, like being betrayed by his jealous brothers and sold into slavery.

Despite these hardships, Joseph remained aligned with the will of God. Even when thrown into prison, he did not lose heart. Instead, he continued to serve others and show kindness, which ultimately led to opportunities in the palace. Joseph's life displayed the characteristics discussed earlier: purity, peaceability, gentleness, willingness to yield, mercy, good fruits, impartiality, and absence of hypocrisy. Without these qualities, his story could have turned out quite differently.

However, there was one final principle Joseph needed to learn, which took an additional two years: interpreting dreams and applying practical solutions to achieve desired outcomes. This lesson became evident in the story of the baker, where Joseph's grace should have enabled him to turn the negative dream into a positive outcome to save the life of the baker. This skill was later employed to interpret Pharaoh's dream and how he employed the grace in him for a positive solution, but it took him an additional two years to learn this.

At times, we may find ourselves held back in order to learn the necessary lessons that God intends for us, much like Joseph's story illustrates. As we continue to grow in our relationship with God and in our respective vocations, regardless of how we entered into our current positions, we have the opportunity to cultivate exceptional wisdom, just as Joseph did. The grace bestowed upon us by God equips and empowers us to transform challenging circumstances into positive outcomes.

Joseph faced significant disadvantages in every human sense. He found himself in the position of a slave, belonging to a minority group as a Jew, and even experienced imprisonment. However, despite these seemingly insurmountable circumstances, Joseph's disadvantaged status became irrelevant when he possessed the crucial answer to the most pressing question in the king's heart.

Through our journey of faith and work, we encounter various trials and obstacles that serve as opportunities for personal and spiritual growth. These experiences shape and refine us, enabling us to develop the wisdom, character, and skills necessary for the tasks and purposes God has ordained for our lives. It is in these moments of difficulty that God often works most profoundly, teaching us valuable lessons that will ultimately reveal His plans and bring forth His blessings.

Joseph's journey exemplifies the significance of holding onto the vision in our hearts, the wisdom in our minds, and the grace bestowed upon us. Despite the trials he faced, Joseph remained steadfast in his vision. Similarly, we have been given a vision for our lives, but God often reveals the process to the ultimate destination incrementally. If Joseph had known he would spend thirteen years in prison before his dreams came to fruition, he might have been discouraged. Yet, he trusted in God's plan.

Likewise, we must trust in God's timing and guidance as we navigate our own journeys. By embracing the vision, wisdom, and grace bestowed upon us, we can experience growth, overcome challenges, and ultimately fulfill our purpose.

In the story of Daniel, we find another example of attaining wealth and success through the corporate ladder, as described in Daniel 6:1-3. Similar to Joseph, Daniel exemplified the elements of wisdom by refusing to defile himself with the king's food. He remained committed to God and chose to abide by godly principles even in a foreign land.

There may be moments in our own lives when we find ourselves as the only Christian in a particular setting, faced with the temptation to compromise our values for personal gain. However, we can take inspiration from Daniel's unwavering stand. Despite the challenges, Daniel trusted in God's nearness and sought His help to overcome temptations. God is always present to assist us when we are willing to yield and ask for His guidance.

By remaining steadfast in our faith, even in difficult circumstances, and upholding godly principles, we position ourselves for success and favour in our professional endeavours. Our commitment to God and adherence to His ways become testimonies of His faithfulness and enable us to navigate the corporate world with integrity and godly wisdom.

In Daniel chapter 1, verse 20, we observe that Daniel, despite being in an environment where he was surrounded by individuals who possessed supernatural powers such as magicians and astrologers, stood out. He surpassed them all by tenfold due to the excellent spirit within him. This principle is applicable to our own employment situations. When we yield to the spirit of God and activate the unique advantage we have through His wisdom, we are never at a disadvantage. By consciously aligning ourselves with God's wisdom and embodying the eight elements of wisdom mentioned earlier, we can excel in our work and rise above any challenges or limitations we may face.

David grew in his employment as we can see from his story. Initially he needed time to enquire of the Lord to interpret dreams and proffer solutions. The first instance is found in Daniel 2:16-18, where King

Nebuchadnezzar had a troubling dream and demanded his wise men to interpret it. Daniel requested time from the king, asking for a respite to seek God's revelation and provide the interpretation. Daniel and his companions prayed, and God revealed the dream and its meaning to Daniel, enabling him to present the interpretation before the king.

However, a time came in his life when he had matured in the things of God that those solutions came immediately, he was faced in with any situation. The second instance is recorded in Daniel 5:13-30, during the reign of King Belshazzar. A mysterious writing appeared on the wall during a great feast, causing the king to become terrified. The wise men were once again unable to interpret the writing. This time, Daniel did not need additional time but immediately offered to interpret the writing on the wall. Through divine insight, Daniel revealed the message and its significance to the astonished king.

In the corporate world, you possess an extraordinary advantage that, when activated, can propel you towards success. Relying solely on human intellect will only take you so far because the challenges and competitions you encounter are not limited to human capabilities alone. To emerge victorious, we must tap into a higher power.

As believers, we have access to divine wisdom and guidance that surpasses human understanding. By aligning ourselves with God's wisdom, seeking His counsel, and relying on His strength, we gain an advantage that transcends mere human capabilities. This advantage enables us to navigate complex situations, make wise decisions, and overcome obstacles that others may struggle with.

To activate this advantage, we must acknowledge our reliance on God and His wisdom. We should seek His direction in every aspect of our professional lives, trusting that He will provide the insight and discernment needed for success. By aligning our thoughts, actions, and decisions with His principles, we position ourselves to make a significant impact in the corporate world.

Remember, the story of Daniel demonstrates that it is not merely our own intellect that will lead us to victory, but our connection to the divine source of wisdom. By embracing this truth, we can confidently face challenges, outshine the competition, and achieve success with a higher purpose in mind.

The final example in this chapter highlights the story of Jacob, who serves as an illustration of being chosen and blessed by God. It is important to recognize that even if Jacob hadn't deceived his father, he would still have been chosen because his selection occurred before his birth. This event is recorded in Genesis 25:23, where Rebecca, Jacob's mother, was pregnant with twins (Jacob and Esau). The verse states, "And the Lord said to her: 'Two nations are in your womb, two peoples shall be separated from your body; one people shall be stronger than the other, and the older shall serve the younger.'"

This principle of being chosen extends to our lives as born-again believers. Peter describes it in 1 Peter 2:9, declaring, "But you are a chosen generation, a royal priesthood, a holy nation, His own special people, that you may proclaim the praises of Him who called you out of darkness into His marvelous light." As part of a chosen and honoured priesthood, you are destined to live a life of royalty.

As a Christian, it is essential to recognize that your faith is not a coincidence. You were chosen before your birth to live a life of purpose, abundance, and wealth in order to fulfill God's divine plan. This truth is evident in the life of Jeremiah as well, as stated in Jeremiah 1:5: "***Before I formed you in the womb I knew you; before you were born I sanctified you; I ordained you a prophet to the nations***."

Understanding our chosen status empowers us to embrace the extraordinary life God has destined for us. It enables us to walk confidently in our calling, knowing that we have been set apart by God Himself. We too can experience the fulfillment of God's plans as we align ourselves with His will.

Jacob served Laban for a total of 20 years. After fleeing from his brother Esau, Jacob arrived in Haran, where he met Laban, his uncle. Jacob agreed to work for Laban in exchange for the hand of his daughter Rachel in marriage. However, Laban deceived Jacob by giving him Leah, Rachel's older sister, as his wife instead. Jacob then had to work an additional seven years to marry Rachel.

During his time with Laban, Jacob worked as a shepherd and tended to Laban's flocks. Over the course of his service, Jacob faced various challenges and experienced blessings from God. He eventually built his own wealth through selective breeding and acquired a significant portion of Laban's livestock.

The final example in this chapter highlights the story of Jacob, who serves as an illustration of being chosen and blessed by God. It is important to recognize that even if Jacob hadn't deceived his father, he would still have been chosen because his selection occurred before his birth. This event is recorded in Genesis 25:23, where Rebecca, Jacob's mother, was pregnant with twins (Jacob and Esau). The verse states, "And the Lord said to her: 'Two nations are in your womb, two peoples shall be separated from your body; one people shall be stronger than the other, and the older shall serve the younger.'"

This principle of being chosen extends to our lives as born-again believers. Peter describes it in 1 Peter 2:9, declaring, "*But you are a chosen generation, a royal priesthood, a holy nation, His own special people, that you may proclaim the praises of Him who called you out of darkness into His marvelous light.*"

As a Christian, it is essential to recognize that your faith is not a coincidence. You were chosen before your birth to live a life of purpose, abundance, and wealth in order to fulfill God's divine plan. This truth is evident in the life of Jeremiah as well, as stated in Jeremiah 1:5: "*Before I formed you in the womb I knew you; before you were born I sanctified you; I ordained you a prophet to the nations.*"

Understanding our chosen status empowers us to embrace the extraordinary life God has destined for us. It enables us to walk confidently in our calling, knowing that we have been set apart by God Himself. Just as Jacob, Peter, and Jeremiah discovered their divine purpose, we too can experience the fulfillment of God's plans as we align ourselves with His will.

Jacob served Laban for a total of 20 years. After fleeing from his brother Esau, Jacob arrived in Haran, where he met Laban, his uncle. Jacob agreed to work for Laban in exchange for the hand of his daughter Rachel in marriage. However, Laban deceived Jacob by giving him Leah, Rachel's older sister, as his wife instead. Jacob then had to work an additional seven years to marry Rachel.

During his time with Laban, Jacob worked as a shepherd and tended to Laban's flocks. Over the course of his service, Jacob faced various challenges and experienced blessings from God. He eventually built his own wealth through selective breeding and acquired a significant portion of Laban's livestock.

You can begin your employment journey in various places, just like Jacob did. What mattered most was his focus and recognition of the grace he carried. The blessing of God was upon him, regardless of whether he worked for a multinational business, a small venture, or even his uncle who had deceived him. As I have emphasized before, we are never at a disadvantage. Jacob remained steadfast and dedicated, exhibiting all the elements of wisdom, diligently working for all those years. His motivation may have varied, but he embraced the opportunity to learn the trade and gain invaluable experience. Eventually, he acquired the knowledge and skills needed to embark on his own business venture.

I often advise those I counsel to view their job responsibilities as preparations for the life God has called them to. It is crucial to absorb all the knowledge and skills available. If you are in sales, consider learning some accounting principles. If you work in customer service, explore acquiring technical skills. Similarly, if you are in a technical field, strive to develop soft skills that will keep you relevant and adaptable for future endeavors when the time comes to pursue your own business or career path.

In line with what we discussed earlier in Chapter 3 of this book, it is important to note that Laban experienced blessings and prosperity due to Jacob's presence. Similarly, we see a similar pattern in the story of Joseph while he served in Potiphar's house.

When individuals with God-given gifts and talents are present in a business or household, their presence can bring blessings and favor to those around them. Jacob's exceptional abilities in animal husbandry contributed to Laban's prosperity. Likewise, Joseph's wisdom and integrity led to the prosperity and success of Potiphar's household.

This reminds us of the significant impact we can have on the environments we find ourselves in. As believers, our presence should bring blessings, wisdom, and favor to the places we work and the people we interact with. It is a testament to the power of God working through us and the influence we can have when we walk in alignment with His principles.

So, whether we are employees, entrepreneurs, or in any other role, let us strive to be conduits of blessings and agents of positive change in the places where we are positioned. Through our dedication, excellence, and alignment with God's purposes, we can make a meaningful difference and contribute to the prosperity of those around us.

Just like Jacob, remember that every experience and skill you acquire in your current employment can serve as a stepping stone toward greater things. Embrace the learning opportunities before you and seize every chance to expand your skill set. The lessons you learn and the wisdom you gain will contribute to your future success.

Eventually in Genesis 30:43, the bible says, *"Thus the man [Jacob] became exceedingly prosperous and had large flocks, female servants and male servants, and camels and donkeys."*

The lives of Joseph, Jacob, and Daniel offer valuable lessons on building wealth through employment and embodying the elements of wisdom. Here are the key lessons we can derive from their stories:

- **Diligence and Hard Work (**Genesis 39:4-6, Daniel 6:3**)**: All three men exemplify the importance of hard work and dedication in their respective employments. They embraced their roles with diligence and consistently gave their best efforts.

- **Integrity and Godly Principles** (Genesis 39:9, Daniel 1:8): Joseph and Daniel refused to compromise their faith and godly principles, even in challenging circumstances. They remained steadfast in their commitment to righteousness and maintained their integrity.

- **Wisdom and Skill Development** (Genesis 30:27-32, Genesis 41: 33-39): Joseph and Jacob displayed wisdom in their business dealings and stewardship of resources. They exhibited astute management skills, strategic thinking, and the ability to seize opportunities.

- **Faithfulness and Favour** (Genesis 39:2-3, Daniel 1:9): Joseph, Jacob, and Daniel experienced God's faithfulness and favor in their careers. They remained faithful to God amidst adversity and were rewarded with favour, promotion, and prosperity.

- **Humility and Dependence on God** (Genesis 41:16, Daniel 2:30): These men recognized that their success was not solely a result of their own efforts but attributed it to God's guidance and provision. They acknowledged their dependence on God and humbly sought His wisdom and direction.

- **Adaptability and Learning** (Genesis 31:6-7): Jacob, in particular, demonstrated the importance of being adaptable and willing to learn. He acquired knowledge and skills while working for Laban, which prepared him for his own business ventures.

- **Vision and Goal Orientation** (Genesis 37:5-10, Genesis 41:32):

Joseph held onto the vision and dreams God had given him, even in the midst of challenging circumstances. He remained focused on his goals and trusted God's plan, which led to his eventual elevation and prosperity.

- **God's Timing and Sovereignty** (Genesis 41:14, 39-40, Daniel 2:21): Throughout their journeys, Joseph, Jacob, and Daniel learned to trust in God's perfect timing and sovereignty. They understood that their success was in God's hands and aligned their lives with His purposes.

Building wealth through Business

Building lasting wealth is often associated with conventional means of building a business, but the Bible reveals that wealth can also be obtained through employment. This principle is exemplified in the lives of Joseph, Daniel and Jacob. For the wealth built through building of business, we will use the lives of Abraham, Isaac, and Job.

Lessons from Job

In the case of Job, the Bible initially does not explicitly mention how he acquired his wealth, only that he was already a wealthy and prosperous man from the east (Job 1:3). However, as Job's story unfolds, we discover that he received seed capital from his family and friends, which multiplied his abundance even more than before.

While the primary lesson from Job's story revolves around trust in God amid suffering, we can discern that his wealth was not solely attributed to what he received, but rather to the evident blessing of God upon his life. Job's increased blessings serve as a testament to God's favour and demonstrate key lessons we can learn from his journey of wealth creation through business.

Please note that Job's story primarily emphasizes trust in God during trials, but we can still derive valuable insights into wealth creation through business from his overall experience.

- **Enduring faith in challenging times**: Job's unwavering faith and perseverance in the face of immense loss and suffering serve as an example of resilience and trust in God's faithfulness (Job 13:15; James 5:11). This reminds us to remain steadfast during economic downturns or setbacks.

- **Trusting in God's guidance and providence**: Job trusted in God's sovereignty and relied on Him for direction and provision (Job 1:21). Acknowledging God as the ultimate source of success and seeking His wisdom and guidance are crucial elements in building a business.

- **Maintaining integrity and righteousness**: Job's commitment to living a blameless and upright life (Job 1:1) serves as a reminder of the importance of ethical conduct in business. Upholding integrity, honesty, and moral values in all aspects of your business dealings is vital for long-term success.

- **Persevering through adversity**: Job's story exemplifies endurance in the face of immense challenges and loss.

Building a business requires resilience and determination to overcome obstacles and setbacks. Trusting in God's faithfulness and remaining steadfast in the midst of trials can lead to eventual restoration and abundance (Job 42:12-13).

- **Cultivating a spirit of generosity**: Job was known for his generosity and willingness to help the needy (Job 29:11-16). Incorporating acts of kindness, philanthropy, and social responsibility into your business model can create a positive impact in society and contribute to long-term success.

- **Surrounding yourself with wise counsel**: Job's friends provided counsel, albeit with mixed results. However, seeking advice from knowledgeable and trustworthy individuals can bring wisdom and fresh perspectives to your business decisions. Proverbs 15:22 emphasizes the importance of seeking counsel, as *"plans fail for lack of counsel, but with many advisers, they succeed."*

- Job's act of praying for his friends carries an important lesson in wealth creation and relationships. Despite enduring immense suffering, Job interceded on behalf of his friends who had wrongly accused and criticized him throughout his trials (Job 42:10). This demonstrates the significance of maintaining healthy relationships, forgiveness, and compassion in the pursuit of wealth and overall well-being.

Lessons from Isaac

Isaac did not only receive gifts from his father Abraham but also the blessing, while the other children from his concubines received material possessions. Isaac was known for his skills in agriculture and farming just like his father Abraham, as he successfully planted crops and reaped a hundredfold harvest, as mentioned in Genesis 26:12. Genesis 26:12-14 recounts the story of Isaac, the son of Abraham, and the blessings and prosperity he received from God:

"Isaac planted crops in that land and the same year reaped a hundredfold, because the Lord blessed him. The man became rich, and his wealth continued to grow until he became very wealthy. He had so many flocks and herds and servants that the Philistines envied him."

Abraham's experience and expertise in managing herds, cultivating land, and dealing with agricultural challenges would have been passed down to Isaac through observation, instruction, and practical involvement in their daily activities. This would have equipped Isaac with the necessary skills and understanding to continue and expand their agricultural endeavours.

However, in Genesis 26, we see that there was a famine in the land, and Isaac could not solely rely on the possessions he received from his father. He had to trust in the God of his father and seek His guidance. When the Philistines closed the wells that he had dug, Isaac did not engage in arguments with them. Instead, he moved on to different locations and dug new wells. He understood that the source of his prosperity was not the physical wells but the blessing and anointing of God upon his life.

Similarly, in your business endeavors, it is crucial to wholeheartedly rely on God for direction. There may be obstacles and opposition along the way, but the results you have achieved thus far can be replicated because the true blessing comes from God. Even if what you currently possess is taken away, God's guidance and favor will continue to lead you to new opportunities and prosperity.

The key lesson from Isaac's experience is to trust in God's provision and guidance, to be adaptable and resilient in the face of challenges, and to recognize that true wealth and success come from the blessings and anointing of God upon your life and business.

From the life of Isaac, there are several lessons we can draw for business success:

- **Faithfulness and obedience (Genesis 26:2-6)**: Isaac demonstrated faithfulness by obeying God's instructions and staying in the land despite the famine. In business, it is essential to be faithful to your commitments, follow ethical principles, and obey God's leading.

- **Perseverance and resilience (Genesis 26:18-22)**: Isaac encountered challenges when the Philistines closed the wells he had dug. Instead of giving up, he persisted and moved on to dig new wells. In business, perseverance and resilience are crucial traits to overcome obstacles and continue pursuing your goals.

- **Trusting in God's provision (26:12-14)**: Isaac relied on God's provision for his success. He recognized that his prosperity came from God's blessing and anointing. Trusting in God's provision and seeking His guidance in your business endeavours can lead to greater success and fulfillment.

- **Negotiation and conflict resolution (Genesis 26:21-22)**: Isaac's willingness to resolve conflicts peacefully with the Philistines by moving to new locations and digging new wells demonstrates the importance of negotiation and conflict resolution skills in business. Finding amicable solutions and maintaining positive relationships can contribute to long-term success.

- **Recognizing and utilizing resources (Genesis 26:12)**: Isaac was skilled in agriculture and understood how to utilize the land's resources for his benefit. In business, recognizing and leveraging available resources, whether it be talents, opportunities, or partnerships, can contribute to growth and success.

Lessons from Abraham

We know Abraham was involved in agriculture and animal husbandry. Throughout his life, he lived as a nomadic herdsman, moving from place to place with his livestock.

We have discussed Abraham's life extensively in this book. We will focus on the lessons from his life here.

- **Vision and Strategy:** Abraham had a vision and a clear sense of purpose. He believed in God's promise of making him a great nation and used his business acumen to strategically acquire wealth and resources (Genesis 13:2). This highlights the significance of having a clear vision, setting goals, and implementing effective strategies in our businesses.

- **God's Covenant and Blessings**: Abraham experienced God's covenant and blessings, including material prosperity and a lasting legacy (Genesis 12:2-3). This reminds us of the importance of seeking God's guidance and relying on His blessings for our business success.

- **Trustworthy Character**: Abraham was regarded as a man of integrity, as demonstrated by his honesty, fairness, and trustworthiness in his interactions with others (Genesis 23:6). This emphasizes the significance of maintaining a good reputation, acting ethically, and building trust in our business relationships.

- **Leaving a legacy**: Abraham's blessings and prosperity extended beyond his lifetime (Genesis 26:23-24). As entrepreneurs, it is important to consider the legacy we leave behind – not just in terms of wealth, but also in terms of values, impact, and inspiring future generations. Proverbs 13:22: *"A good man leaves an inheritance to his children's children." (NKJV).*

The strategies for generating wealth, as explored in this chapter, can only yield results when implemented wholeheartedly, in conjunction with the concept of positioning oneself in the specific location where God intends to bless them, as discussed in chapter two of this book. Receiving guidance from God is of utmost importance when it comes to operating in His blessings. It is through hearing from Him that you will discover the specific job or business that aligns with His plan for your life. This truth is beautifully expressed in Isaiah 30:21 (KJV): **"And thine ears shall hear a word behind thee, saying, This is the way, walk ye in it, when ye turn to the right hand, and when ye turn to the left."**

CHAPTER SIX

WHY GOD WANT YOU TO BE WEALTHY

CHAPTER SIX
WHY GOD WANT YOU TO BE WEALTHY

Throughout the various chapters of this book, we have presented evidence supporting the notion that it is part of God's plan for us to experience wealth. Now, the question arises: "Why does God desire us to be wealthy?"

Similar to many other principles found in the Bible, the concept of wealth creation presents us with a choice. One can opt to believe that wealth is not meant for them and still lead a fulfilling life both in this world and in the world to come. It is important to note that being wealthy does not determine one's ultimate success in life. However, it is advantageous to be wealthy as it can facilitate a more comfortable existence. With financial resources at hand, one can focus on matters that hold genuine significance rather than being preoccupied by financial burdens.

Before we delve into the reasons why God desires us to be wealthy, let us first consider the benefits of wealth. While wealth should not be our sole pursuit, it can greatly enhance our quality of life. It provides us with the means to meet our basic needs, pursue our passions, and positively impact the lives of others through acts of generosity and compassion.

Now, let us explore the reasons why God desires us to experience wealth.

While the focus is not necessarily on being wealthy for the sake of wealth itself, there are principles and guidance that can help Christians navigate wealth in a way that aligns with their faith and serves a greater purpose. Here are some key points, along with relevant Bible references:

- **Stewardship and Responsibility**: Christians are called to be faithful stewards of the resources and blessings entrusted to them. This includes wealth and financial resources. In Luke 12:48, Jesus teaches that "from everyone who has been given much, much will be demanded; and from the one who has been entrusted with much, much more will be asked." This implies that having wealth comes with the responsibility to use it wisely for the glory of God and the well-being of others. In Matthew 25:14-30: The parable of the talents emphasizes the importance of being faithful stewards of the resources entrusted to us, including wealth.

- **Generosity and Giving**: Wealth can be an opportunity to practice generosity and contribute to the needs of others. Proverbs 11:25 states, "A generous person will prosper; whoever refreshes others will be refreshed." By using wealth to bless and support others, Christians can participate in God's work of bringing about justice and helping the less fortunate.

  - Acts 4:32-37: The early Christians shared their possessions and resources with one another, demonstrating a spirit of generosity and care for those in need.
  - 2 Corinthians 8:1-5: The Macedonian churches, despite their own poverty, generously

gave to support the needs of others.

- **Avoiding the Love of Money**: While wealth itself is not condemned, the Bible warns against the love of money and the pursuit of wealth as an idol. In 1 Timothy 6:10, it is written, "For the love of money is a root of all kinds of evil. Some people, eager for money, have wandered from the faith and pierced themselves with many griefs." Christians are called to prioritize their relationship with God above worldly wealth, recognizing that true fulfillment and contentment come from Him. In Luke 12:13-21: Jesus tells the parable of the rich fool, warning against greed and the accumulation of wealth without considering one's spiritual well-being.

- **Contentment and Trust in God**: The
  Bible encourages contentment and
  trust in God's provision, regardless of
  one's wealth or financial status. In
  Philippians 4:11-12, the Apostle Paul
  writes, "I have learned to be content
  whatever the circumstances. I know
  what it is to be in need, and I know
  what it is to have plenty. I have
  learned the secret of being content in
  any and every situation, whether well
  fed or hungry, whether living in plenty
  or in want." This highlights the
  importance of finding satisfaction in
  Christ rather than solely in material
  possessions.
    - Philippians 4:11-13: The Apostle
      Paul expresses his contentment
      in all circumstances,
      acknowledging that his strength

and satisfaction come from Christ.

- o 1 Timothy 6:6-8: Paul emphasizes that godliness with contentment is great gain, as we brought nothing into the world and will take nothing out of it.

- **Using Wealth for Kingdom Purposes**: Christians are encouraged to use their wealth to advance God's kingdom and promote His values. In Matthew 6:19-20, Jesus advises, "Do not store up for yourselves treasures on earth, where moths and vermin destroy, and where thieves break in and steal. But store up for yourselves treasures in heaven, where moths and vermin do not destroy, and where thieves do not break in and steal." This implies investing in eternal matters and using resources to further God's work on Earth.

- o Matthew 6:19-21: Jesus encourages storing up treasures in heaven rather than focusing solely on earthly possessions.
- o Luke 19:1-10: The story of Zacchaeus demonstrates the transformative power of using wealth for good, as he commits to giving half of his possessions to the poor and making amends for his wrongs.

CHAPTER SEVEN

THE

COVENANT

OF GIVING

CHAPTER SEVEN
THE COVENANT OF GIVING

The covenant of giving is an essential aspect of building lasting wealth as a Christian. It signifies the trust and relationship between God and man, and it is evident throughout the Bible. God, as the ultimate giver, has blessed us with life and every good thing we enjoy. He only asks us to give back as a demonstration of our trust in Him. We demonstrate our trust in God when we become comfortable when the topic of giving is being discussed.

Abraham serves as a model of faith and wealth creation. Although God promised to bless him, He never required Abraham to give anything in return but for him to obey. However, when Abraham willingly obeyed and followed God's command to sacrifice

Isaac, God reaffirmed His promise and expanded it in Genesis 22:16-18. He assured Abraham of abundant blessings, numerous descendants, victory over enemies, and a role in blessing all nations.

Just as Abraham's faith was tested through the sacrifice of Isaac, our giving involves sacrificing our resources. One may question if Abraham truly sacrificed Isaac, but in a sense, he did. Similarly, when we sacrifice our money and resources, we also experience a form of sacrifice. However, the beauty lies in the fact that when we willingly give and let go, we receive them back in abundance. However, when we give, we receive abundantly in return. Luke 6:38 echoes this principle: "**Give, and it shall be given unto you; good measure, pressed down, and shaken together, and running over, shall men give into your bosom. For** *with the same measure that ye mete withal it shall be measured to you again.*"

Therefore, understanding the covenant of giving and embracing it is crucial for building lasting wealth. It is a reflection of our trust in God's provision and a pathway to experience His blessings overflowing in our lives.

The subject of sacrificial giving is does not have dichotomy between old and new testaments. When one starts debating whether a particular giving is relating to the old or new testament, just know that they have not really understood the subject of giving. There are three avenue that the Bible shows for us to give. They include giving to God, giving to the prophet, and giving to the poor.

Giving to God

Our first gift to God is ourselves. This is the subject we have attempted to describe throughout this book by how we live. We are the first sacrifice. Romans 12:1, "*I appeal to you therefore, brothers and sisters, by the mercies of God, to present your bodies as a living sacrifice, holy and acceptable to God, which is your spiritual worship.*" Here, the apostle Paul encourages believers to offer themselves wholly to God, dedicating their lives as a sacrifice in service to Him. This signifies the surrender of our desires, ambitions, and willto align with God's purposes, allowing Him to work through us for His glory.

Haven established that, there are specific giving that the bible commands.

Tithes

The foundation of the tithe is rooted in the Old Testament of the Bible, specifically in the Mosaic Law given to the Israelites. The command to tithe was established as part of the covenant between God and His chosen people.

The first mention of tithing in the Bible can be found in Genesis 14:18-20, when Abraham encountered Melchizedek, the king of Salem and a priest of God. Abraham gave a tenth of all the spoils of war to Melchizedek. This act of tithing is seen as an act of worship and recognition of God's provision and blessing.

The practice of tithing was later incorporated into the Mosaic Law given through Moses. In the book of Leviticus, specifically Leviticus 27:30, the Israelites were commanded to bring a tithe, or a tenth, of their produce and livestock to support the Levites, who served in the tabernacle or temple, and to provide for the needs of the poor and needy.

Tithing continued to be emphasized throughout the Old Testament, and it served as a way for the Israelites to demonstrate their obedience to God and acknowledge His provision in their lives. It was a foundational principle in their worship and stewardship of the resources entrusted to them.

It is important to note that while the principle of tithing was given in the Old Testament, the New Testament does not explicitly command Christians to tithe. However, One instance where Jesus mentioned tithing is found in Matthew 23:23, where He rebuked the Pharisees, who were meticulous in tithing even the smallest herbs, but neglected justice, mercy, and faithfulness. Jesus affirmed the importance of tithing but emphasized that it should not overshadow the weightier matters of the law.

It is important to highlight that Jesus' comment does not imply that the subject is no longer relevant. Rather, it emphasizes that there are more significant matters within the law. Additionally, it is worth remembering that tithing was practiced by Abraham even before the law was established. Therefore, even if one believes that certain aspects of the law have been abolished, tithing remains significant as it predates the law itself. Tithing serves as a means to honour God, support the work of the church, and demonstrate our trust in God's provision.

In the New Testament, Melchizedek is primarily referenced in the book of Hebrews, where he is portrayed as a type or foreshadowing of Jesus Christ. The author of Hebrews draws parallels between Melchizedek and Jesus, highlighting their unique and elevated roles as both priests and kings.

Melchizedek is described as being without a father or mother, without genealogy, having neither the beginning of days nor end of life. This portrayal is symbolic and signifies his eternal nature and his representation of a different, superior priesthood. The author of Hebrews emphasizes that Melchizedek's priesthood is greater than that of the Levitical priesthood, which was established under the Mosaic law.

The comparison between Melchizedek and Jesus serves to illustrate the superiority of Jesus' priesthood over the Levitical priesthood. It supports the author's argument that Jesus, as the ultimate high priest, has brought about a new and better covenant between God and humanity.

Bible references - Hebrews 5:6, Hebrews 5:10, Hebrews 6:20, Hebrews 7:1-3, Hebrews 7:11

Abraham faithfully paid his tithe to Melchizedek, and Jesus is forever in that same priestly order. I strongly advocate for the practice of tithing, and when God led me on the path of wealth creation through biblical principles, He emphasized the importance of aligning my finances through tithes, offerings, and firstfruits. Personally, I had stopped tithing for about five years before this transformative encounter.

If you find yourself still debating with God about money matters, it could be a sign that He is calling you on this journey and desires for you to experience financial prosperity. The sooner you obey, the sooner you can embark on this path. Giving will never be comfortable, as true giving requires sacrifice. Just as Abraham faced the challenge of sacrificing his son, it was not an easy task. In 2 Samuel 24:24 (NKJV), David declared that he would not offer anything to the Lord that did not cost him anything: *"Then the king said to Araunah, 'No, but I will surely buy it from you for a price; nor will I offer burnt offerings to the LORD my God with that which costs me nothing.' So David bought the threshing floor and the oxen for fifty shekels of silver*."

Let us remember that giving involves a genuine sacrifice, and it is through this sacrificial act that we honor God and experience His blessings in our lives.

Who You Should Pay Your Tithe To

While it may seem obvious to say that you should pay your tithe to your pastor, I've encountered many people who challenge this and claim they can pay it to whoever they want. When there is a disagreement or question about a doctrine in the Bible, one method of resolving it is through the law of first mention. This involves going back to the initial mention of the doctrine, which sets the foundation for its subsequent understanding and application. As we have established, in Genesis 14:18-20, Abraham first paid tithe to Melchizedek, who we agree is Jesus in our case. Another reference can be found in Leviticus 27:30, which states: **"A tithe of everything from the land, whether grain from the soil or fruit from the trees, belongs to the LORD; it is holy to the LORD."**

Having established that our tithe is first paid to God and is holy, the question arises as to which human vessel we should pay it to. The answer can be found in Numbers 18:21, which states: *"To the Levites I have given every tithe in Israel for an inheritance, in return for their service that they do, their service in the tent of meeting."* This indicates that the tithe was given to the Levites, who were responsible for serving in the tabernacle and conducting religious activities. The tithes provided for the livelihood and sustenance of the Levites, as they did not receive a land inheritance like the other tribes of Israel.

Another reference, Malachi 3:10, states: *"Bring the full tithe into the storehouse, that there may be food in my house. And thereby put me to the test, says the LORD of hosts, if I will not open the windows of heaven for you and pour down for you a blessing until there is no more need*." The purpose of bringing the full tithe into the storehouse was to ensure an abundance of food in the house of God. The tithes were meant to support the needs of the priests, Levites, and the maintenance of the tabernacle or temple.

Based on the above, it is clear that we must pay our tithe to the house of God. If you belong to a local church, that is where you should pay it. This act demonstrates your commitment to the church, which serves as your spiritual home and provides nourishment. If you still have doubts about where to pay your tithe, ask God for guidance instead of seeking the advice of others. He will direct you appropriately. I have heard stories of people who pay their tithe to the poor or distribute it to different churches, but this practice does not align with the teachings of the Bible. While you may give offerings to support other causes or provide alms to the poor, your tithe must be paid to your local assembly.

Offerings

These are voluntary gifts given above and beyond tithes. They can be presented in worship, gratitude, or support for specific purposes. In 2 Corinthians 9:7, believers are instructed to give as they have decided in their hearts, not reluctantly or under compulsion, for God loves a cheerful giver.

The foundation of offering in the Bible is rooted in the concept of giving back to God a portion of what He has blessed us with. Offering is an act of voluntary giving that goes beyond the mandatory tithe. It is an expression of gratitude, worship, and faithfulness to God.

Offering remains important today because it fosters a spirit of generosity, cultivates a heart of gratitude, and aligns our priorities with God's kingdom. It allows us to actively participate in God's work and experience the joy of giving as we impact the lives of others and honor God with our resources. Offering is important for several reasons:

- **Worship and Honour (Proverbs 3:9)**: Offering is a way to honour God and acknowledge His sovereignty over our lives. It is an act of worship, where we present our gifts to God as a symbol of our love, devotion, and gratitude.

- **Trust and Dependency (Philippians 4:19)**: Offering reflects our trust in God's provision. By willingly giving a portion of our resources, we demonstrate our reliance on Him as our ultimate provider. It is an act of faith that God will continue to provide for our needs as we prioritize His kingdom.

- **Kingdom Advancement (Acts 2:45)**: Offering supports the work of God's kingdom on earth. It enables the ministry and missions to reach out, spread the Gospel, meet the needs of others, and make a positive impact in the world. Through our offerings, we participate in God's redemptive plan and contribute to the growth and expansion of His kingdom.

- **Generosity and Blessing**: Offering is an opportunity to demonstrate generosity. The Bible teaches that those who give generously will be blessed abundantly in return (2 Corinthians 9:6-8).

- **Attitude of the Heart (2 Corinthians 9:7 and Luke 6:38)**: Offering is not just about the amount we give but also about the attitude of our hearts. God looks at our motives and the condition of our hearts when we give. It is an opportunity for self-examination, humility, and alignment with God's purposes.

Firstfruits

This refers to dedicating the first portion of one's harvest or income to God. Proverbs 3:9-10 encourages honouring the Lord with the firstfruits of all one's produce and acknowledging Him with the best of one's possessions.

The origin of the concept of firstfruits can be traced back to agricultural practices in ancient times. In agricultural societies, the firstfruits referred to the initial and best portion of the harvest that was dedicated or offered to God as an expression of gratitude, acknowledgment, and trust in His provision. It symbolized the recognition that all blessings and abundance come from God.

In Leviticus 23:9-14, the Lord instructed the Israelites regarding the offering of the firstfruits: *"When you enter the land I am going to give you and you reap its harvest, bring to the priest a sheaf of the first grain you harvest. He is to wave the sheaf before the Lord so it will be accepted on your behalf; the priest is to wave it on the day after the Sabbath... From the day after the Sabbath, the day you brought the sheaf of the wave offering, count off seven full weeks. Count off fifty days up to the day after the seventh Sabbath, and then present an offering of new grain to the Lord.*"

Firstfruits held a significant cultural and religious significance in the Old Testament. It represented the beginning and the promise of the entire harvest to follow. By offering the firstfruits, people demonstrated their faith in God's faithfulness to continue providing for their needs.

In addition to the agricultural context, the concept of firstfruits also extended beyond crops. It was applied to other areas of life, such as livestock and even human offspring. The principle was to consecrate and dedicate the first and best to God, acknowledging His ownership and sovereignty.

In the New Testament, the concept of firstfruits takes on a spiritual meaning. It is associated with the resurrection of Jesus Christ, who is referred to as the "firstfruits of those who have fallen asleep" in 1 Corinthians 15:20. This signifies that Jesus' resurrection guarantees the future resurrection of believers.

Today, the importance of firstfruits remains relevant in a symbolic and spiritual sense. While the agricultural aspect may not be as prominent in modern societies, the principle of offering the first and best to God still holds significance. It is a way to express gratitude, trust, and worship, acknowledging that everything we have comes from God. Offering our first and best fruits, whether it be our time, resources, talents, or finances, is a way to honor God and prioritize Him in our lives.

Moreover, the concept of firstfruits reminds us of the hope and assurance we have in the resurrection of Jesus Christ. Just as Jesus was the first to rise from the dead, we have the confidence that we too will experience resurrection and eternal life through Him.

Firstfruits continue to be important today as a spiritual principle that encourages believers to give generously, prioritize God in all aspects of life, and have faith in His provision and promises. It is a practice rooted in gratitude, trust, and worship, acknowledging that everything we have comes from God.

Other types of giving to God include Pledge, Vow and Sacrificial giving. Sacrificial Giving involves giving sacrificially, going above and beyond regular giving. In Mark 12:41-44, Jesus commends the widow who gave all she had, highlighting the value of sacrificial giving. it is not necessarily a type of giving but the means by which we give our offering. While we can give our regular offering, Jesus encourages us to give sacrificially.

Pledges can also be considered a form of giving to God. A pledge is a voluntary commitment made by an individual or a community to contribute a specific amount of money or resources over a period of time towards a particular cause or project in support of God's work. However, it is important to note that pledges should be made with careful consideration and sincerity, and they should not be made under compulsion or pressure. Jesus emphasizes the importance of integrity and honesty in our commitments in Matthew 5:37, saying, "Let your 'Yes' be 'Yes,' and your 'No,' 'No.'"

For example, in the Old Testament, individuals made pledges to provide materials for the construction of the tabernacle (Exodus 35:21-22) or to support the Levites in their service (Nehemiah 10:32-39).

Pledges are commonly used in fundraising campaigns or initiatives within religious organizations. On the other hand, a vow is a solemn promise or commitment made to God, usually related to personal conduct, behaviour, or a specific action. Vows often carry a more profound and personal significance, encompassing spiritual, moral, or ethical aspects. Vows are typically focused on one's relationship with God and are often made during significant life events or in response to specific circumstances. For example, Hannah made a vow to God, promising to dedicate her son Samuel to His service (1 Samuel 1:11). Additionally, individuals in the Old Testament made vows to God in times of distress or as an act of devotion.

While both pledges and vows involve commitments to God, vows tend to be more personal and encompass a broader scope of one's life and actions. Pledges, on the other hand, are typically more specific and focused on financial or material contributions.

Giving to the Prophet

Giving to the prophet is not an act of human worship but rather a hidden key that leads you to a place of abundance. In 2 Chronicles 20:20 (KJV), it is written, "And they rose early in the morning and went forth into the wilderness of Tekoa: and as they went forth, Jehoshaphat stood and said, Hear me, O

Judah, and ye inhabitants of Jerusalem; Believe in the LORD your God, so shall ye be established; believe his prophets, so shall ye prosper."

Furthermore, we find in Hosea 12:13 a testament that states, "And by a prophet, the LORD brought Israel out of Egypt, and by a prophet, was he preserved."

While it is true that there are those who may not hold this belief, their skepticism does not diminish the truth presented here. If you encounter anyone who has attained wealth through the principles discussed in this book, they will undoubtedly affirm and disclose this vital truth and secret.

In the Bible, giving to the prophet refers to the act of providing support, assistance, or offerings to those who were recognized as prophets or individuals serving in prophetic roles. Throughout the Old Testament, prophets played a crucial role in delivering God's messages, offering guidance, and proclaiming His will to the people.

There however, two significant accounts in the Bible that highlights the impact of giving to a Prophet.

The first in the story of the Widow and Elijah: In 1 Kings 17:7-16, the prophet Elijah encountered a widow from Zarephath during a time of severe drought and famine. As Elijah approached the widow, he requested a drink of water and also asked her to bring him a morsel of bread. The widow, facing a desperate situation herself, explained that she had only a handful of flour and a little oil left, barely enough to make a final meal for herself and her son before they anticipated starvation.

However, Elijah, acting as a prophet of God, assured the widow that she need not fear. He conveyed to her that by giving a portion of her limited resources to him, it would release a blessing from God upon her and her household.

The widow, despite her dire circumstances, chose to trust in the words of the prophet and display an act of faith through her giving. She offered the small portion of her remaining food to Elijah, demonstrating her obedience and belief in the promise of God's provision.

As a result of her act of giving, God intervened miraculously. The widow's jar of flour and jug of oil were not depleted but continued to provide sustenance for her and her household throughout the entirety of the drought.

This story highlights the principle that giving to a prophet, in obedience and faith, can lead to the release of God's blessings and provision in our lives. The widow's act of giving, although seemingly insignificant in the face of scarcity, opened the door for God's supernatural provision to flow into her life.

The second and most profound is that of Isaac and Esau's Offering: In Genesis 27, Isaac, nearing old age, desired to bless his son Esau before his death. Isaac believed that the blessing held significant power and significance, and he intended to bestow it upon Esau. As part of the blessing process, Isaac requested that Esau go out and hunt game, prepare a savory meal, and bring it to him. Isaac believed that by partaking in this meal, he would be able to release the blessing upon Esau.

The specific nature of the offering, in this case, was crucial to Isaac. He believed that the taste and aroma of the meal prepared by Esau would contribute to the tradition of passing on the blessing. Isaac wanted to experience the sensory elements associated with Esau's offering, which played a symbolic role in the transference of the blessing.

These stories serve as reminders of the power of giving and the faith and obedience it requires for the release of the blessing.

The concept of giving to the prophet is seen in various instances, highlighting the importance of supporting those who were called to be messengers of God. Here are a few examples:

- **Hospitality and Provision**: In 2 Kings 4:8-10, a woman from Shunem showed hospitality to the prophet Elisha by providing a room for him to stay whenever he passed through her town. She and her husband also prepared meals for him, recognizing his role as a servant of God. The woman from Shunem took the initiative in her actions, guided by her perception that Elisha was a servant of God. As the story progresses, we witness how her act of hospitality and faith sparked a divine anointing in Elisha. Through this anointing, he prophesied a remarkable fulfillment of her deepest desire – to bear a son, despite her barrenness.

However, the story takes another unforeseen turn when her son tragically passes away. Yet, even in the face of this heartbreaking loss, the woman's unwavering faith and trust in God's power and Elisha's connection with Him are displayed. Through Elisha's intervention and the working of God's miraculous power, her son is raised back to life.

- **Offerings and Gifts**: Prophets were sometimes recipients of offerings or gifts from individuals or communities. In 1 Kings 14:3-4, Jeroboam's wife was instructed by her husband to take specific gifts when she sought prophet Ahijah advice. This was a customary practice to honour the prophet and seek divine guidance.

- **Financial Support**: In the New Testament, the apostle Paul mentions the principle of providing financial support to those engaged in ministry, including prophets. In 1 Corinthians 9:11, he states, *"If we have sown spiritual things among you, is it too* *much if we reap material things from you?".*

Giving to the Poor

Giving to the poor is a prominent theme in the Bible, emphasizing the importance of generosity, compassion, and care for those in need. The Scriptures contain numerous passages that highlight God's concern for the poor and the responsibility of believers to extend help and support to them. Here are a few key aspects of giving to the poor as presented in the Bible:

- **Compassion for the Poor**: The Bible repeatedly calls for compassion towards the poor, recognizing their vulnerability and need for assistance. Proverbs 19:17 states, "*Whoever is generous to* *the poor lends to the Lord, and he will repay him for his deed*." This verse emphasizes that acts of giving to the poor are seen as acts of service to God Himself. It reminds us that when we extend help to those in need, we are engaging in a sacred duty. Furthermore, it is important to note that God does not owe anything to anyone, for when we lend to others in kindness, it is eventually God who blesses and rewards our benevolent actions.

- **Sharing with the Needy**: The early Christian community exemplified the practice of sharing resources and meeting the needs of the poor. Acts 2:44-45 describe the believers as having "all things in common" and being willing to sell their possessions to provide for those who lacked.

- **The Principle of Gleaning**: In the Old Testament, God instructed the Israelites to leave a portion of their harvest for the poor to glean from. This practice ensured that those in need had access to food and sustenance (Leviticus 23:22; Deuteronomy 24:19-22).

- **Generosity and Blessing**: Proverbs 22:9 teaches that *"Whoever has a bountiful eye will be blessed, for he shares his bread with the poor."* This verse emphasizes the reciprocal relationship between generosity towards the poor and experiencing God's blessings.

- **Caring for Widows and Orphans**: James 1:27 highlights the importance of pure and undefiled religion, which includes visiting and caring for widows and orphans in their distress. This verse underscores the need for practical support and care for the most vulnerable members of society.

- **Christ's Example**: Jesus Himself exemplified compassion for the poor and marginalized, teaching His followers to love their neighbours and extend help to those in need. In Matthew 25:35-40, Jesus identifies Himself with the hungry, thirsty, naked, and imprisoned, emphasizing that acts of kindness towards them are acts of service to Him.

Giving to the poor is regarded as a fundamental expression of faith and obedience to God's commandments. The Bible calls believers to demonstrate love, kindness, and generosity towards those in need, recognizing the inherent dignity and worth of every individual. By giving to the poor, believers have the opportunity to reflect God's heart of compassion and contribute to building a more just and caring society.

One crucial lesson to learn about giving is that there is always something we can give. This principle is exemplified in the story of the widow encountered by the prophet Elisha in 2 Kings 4:1-7. The important lesson to take from this account is that there is always something we can give, even when we perceive it as little. In the story of the widow with the jar of oil, she believed she had nothing except that small jar. However, she offered it willingly, and through a miracle, it became more than enough to resolve her financial difficulties.

Similarly, in Jesus' teaching in Matthew 25:29 (RSV), "*For to everyone who has will more be given, and he will have abundance; but from him who has not, even what he has will be taken away*." He emphasizes that those who have something and use it wisely will receive even more no matter the size. The key is not the size or magnitude of what we have to give, but rather the willingness and faithfulness to offer it with a generous heart.

These examples remind us that every act of giving, no matter how small it may seem, can have a significant impact. Whether it is our time, resources, talents, or even a kind word or gesture, we always have something to offer to others. Our willingness to give, regardless of the perceived magnitude, can bring blessings and make a positive difference in the lives of those around us.

In conclusion, the covenant of giving is an enduring aspect of our relationship with God that transcends the fluctuations of time. Just as God created humanity as male and female, the principle of giving remains a fundamental part of our spiritual journey. It is independent of the ever-evolving debates and discussions surrounding it. The significance of giving persists, unaffected by the shifting tides of societal opinions.

It is worth noting that embracing the principles of giving not only yields earthly rewards but also holds the promise of eternal blessings. By faithfully practicing generosity, we align ourselves with God's purposes and open ourselves to the abundance of His provision. The rewards of giving extend beyond the temporal realm, encompassing the everlasting joy and fulfillment found in God's kingdom.

The covenant of giving stands as a testament to God's unchanging nature and His desire for His children to experience the blessings that come from a generous heart. As we embark on this journey of giving, let us remember that it is not only a means of earthly provision but also a pathway to spiritual growth and an investment in the eternal rewards that await us.

I passionately believe that according to the Bible, there is no such thing as wasteful giving. It does not matter whether you were coerced into giving or not, or whether the recipient appreciated it or not. What matters is the act of giving itself, as it aligns with the principles of love, compassion, and obedience to God's word. Ecclesiastes 11:1 (KJV) beautifully expresses this sentiment:

"Cast thy bread upon the waters: for thou shalt find it after many days."

My prayer for you today is that you may receive a bountiful harvest from all the generous contributions you have made, whether in monetary form, time, or any other valuable resource. May the blessings of your giving overflow abundantly in the name of Jesus.

ABOUT THE BOOK

In the book "Beyond Economics: Unlocking Lasting Wealth With Bible Wisdom" readers will embark on a transformative journey towards understanding and unlocking the true path to lasting wealth. This groundbreaking book challenges conventional economic principles and reveals the hidden secrets that God intends for His followers to discover.

The chapters within this enlightening work delve into essential aspects of wealth creation, providing a comprehensive framework for readers to navigate and implement in their own lives. The foundational principles of wealth creation are explored, laying a solid groundwork for the subsequent chapters.

Readers will then be introduced to the concept of positioning oneself for wealth. Chapter two delves into the significance of aligning oneself with the location and opportunities that God intends to bless. By understanding and embracing this positioning, readers can tap into the divine flow of abundance and experience true prosperity.

Chapter three presents essential principles to wealth creation, offering practical examples on obedience, importance of relationship, and the power of prophecy. These principles are backed by timeless wisdom and proven strategies that have withstood the test of time.

The journey continues with chapter four, which unravels the Eight Elements of Wisdom. These elements provide a holistic approach to wealth creation, incorporating spiritual, emotional, and intellectual aspects that are essential for building enduring prosperity.

The heart of the book lies in chapter five, where the vehicles for wealth creation are explored. Here, readers will discover unconventional approaches that challenge traditional economic principles. By stepping outside the confines of conventional wisdom, readers can uncover new opportunities and possibilities for wealth generation.

"Why God Wants You To Be Wealthy" is the thought-provoking focus of chapter six. Delving into the spiritual aspect of wealth, this chapter reveals divine intentions and the inherent connection between faith and prosperity. Readers will gain a deeper understanding of their divine purpose and the role wealth plays in fulfilling it.

Finally, the book concludes with chapter seven, illuminating the covenant of giving. Exploring the profound impact of generosity and stewardship, readers will learn how giving can activate a cycle of blessings and abundance. This chapter delves into the transformative power of generosity and the significance it holds in building lasting wealth.

"Beyond Economics: Unlocking Lasting Wealth With Bible Wisdom" offers a fresh perspective on wealth creation, intertwining practical wisdom with spiritual principles. This book challenges readers to reevaluate their approach to wealth, daring to venture beyond economic norms and embrace divine insights. Whether you are seeking financial freedom, a deeper spiritual connection, or a purpose-driven life, this book will empower you to uncover the secrets to building lasting wealth, guided by God's wisdom.

ABOUT THE AUTHOR

Ephraim Unuigbe is a distinguished professional with expertise in finance and accounting. As a chartered accountant and a seasoned career and personal finance coach, he brings a wealth of knowledge and experience to his work. Ephraim holds a BSc in Accounting and is a proud member of the Institute of Chartered Accountants of Nigeria. He has also obtained certification as a Certified Information Systems Auditor from the prestigious Information Systems Audit and Control Association.

In addition to his accomplishments in the financial realm, Ephraim is a dedicated minister of the gospel in the Redeemed Christian Church of God (RCCG). Within the church, he serves as a prominent figure in the prayer and evangelism ministry based in

Southampton. His devotion to spiritual matters is complemented by his role as an ordained minister.

While excelling in his professional and religious pursuits, Ephraim is actively engaged in various community and educational initiatives. He is employed at a prominent accounting firm in the United Kingdom, where he provides invaluable assurance services to corporate entities. Furthermore, Ephraim serves as the Director of Corporate Governance on the board of HACTRI, an esteemed Nigerian literacy organization. Additionally, he holds a position as a board member at the Itchen Sixth Form College in the United Kingdom, where he contributes his expertise and guidance.

Beyond his professional and community endeavours, Ephraim finds joy in his personal life. He is happily married to Marian Unuigbe, and together they cherish the blessings of parenthood with their two children, Eseohen Elizabeth and Daniel Chukwudi. Ephraim's commitment to family and faith underpins his unwavering dedication to helping others achieve financial success and spiritual fulfillment.

Acknowledgement

My most important companion, counselor, helper, intercessor, advocate, strengthener, and standby, the Holy Spirit. Thank you.

Other Books by the Author to date

1. Succeeding in your career - A Roadmap for Graduates & Young Professionals
2. Let's talk about money - A guide to Personal Finances for Young Adults
3. How to choose a career path - A Spiritual Perspective to Career Choice & Life.
4. The Career Woman's Guide to SINGLE PARENTING: For Single Female Career Professionals with teenage kids between the ages of 12 -19.
5. Understanding investment for beginners
6. Managing Family Finance - for Career Couples
7. Career & Romance - How to Find Your Soul Mate as a Single Career Professional
8. Understanding accounting for non-accountants
9. The Essential Handbook for Starting a Food, Flower, Retail, Coffee Shop Business.
10. How to be a good person for Children
11. Smart Money: A Guide to Financial Literacy for Children
12. MASTERING INTERVIEWS: 31 Common Interview Questions and Unique Answers, Including Scenario-Based Questions (And bonus answer for how to answer questions about experiences or skills not listed on your CV)
13. Finding Your Purpose: Lessons from The Life and Teachings of Paul

SERVICES WE OFFER
Career Counselling
We assist individuals of all ages in the clarity and attainment of their career goals, and we also teach students the development of learner-centered skills they can utilize in their academic career and life beyond.

Personal Finance Coaching
Personal finance refers to how well people adhere to a budget when managing their finances. Over time, the goal is to save money, while also spending money on resources that are needed and allocating a particular amount for each living expense. With my guidance, you will learn how to make, manage, and multiply your money.

CV Review and Writing
The modern world of employment demands that your CV stands out, and we provide a range of services through which our professional CV writers can create the CV just for you. Every CV we create is tailored specifically to meet your needs.

Cover Letter and Personal Statement
We will provide you with a professional who knows how to write you a high-performing letter for your job application or personal statement. Paired with our professionally written CV you can differentiate yourself from other applicants.

LinkedIn Profile Optimisation
You can take your LinkedIn profile to the next level and turn it into a powerful career tool that highlights your abilities, experiences, and impresses your network of contacts.

Interview Coaching

Our professionals help you be the best candidate your potential employer has ever seen. A well-rounded approach that addresses the verbal and non-verbal factors.

All available on amazon.com and www.ephraim-unuigbe.com

Contact the author via info@ephraim-unuigbe.com

Ephraim™
Unuigbe